CW01627813

ADV[illegible] E

"*The Play Book* clearly presents the case for all adults to return to a state of childhood play — not only because it is good for you but because it is FUN, dammit. The same could be said for *The Play Book* itself: Janet's play manifesto is a "tool book" full of useful tips and resources that are "good for you," and it really is a fun, fast-paced read. So get off your butt and read this book ... or better yet, put the book down and get out and play (but make a plan to read the book later)."

Brian Shelley, Chief Executive & Philanthropy Officer, United Way Simcoe Muskoka, Full-time playmate/dad to two growing boys

"In *The Play Book*, Janet provides a compelling alternative to the notion of dreaded workouts and boring gym time as the only way to achieve long-term health and vitality. Starting with just five minutes a day, Janet demonstrates how easy it can be to add a little fun and variety to our daily routines to help keep us physically — and mentally — healthy."

***Peter Neal, Co-founder of Neal Brothers Foods and Co-author of* Goodness: Recipes & Stories**

"I loved *The Play Book*! It is sound, practical advice that not only lays out the benefits of exercise but also guides each individual through a refreshing perspective on physical well-being. For the beginner or the elite athlete, the bottom line is exercise equals joy, and Janet finds a way to deliver an intricate concept in an engaging and concise manner."

Tracy Wilson, Olympic Bronze Medalist, 3x World Medalist, CTV/TSN, NBC Universal Skating Analyst, and Coach of Olympic and World Champions

"The hardest part of any new job or task is starting it! Janet has delivered a simple yet impactful, inspiring yet relatable game plan for starting the job of looking after the person that matters most: you! By putting everyday life and play in a new context, she enables the reader with a roadmap to get started and to keep on making healthy choices and living a more rewarding life. This simple, easy-to-read perspective is a must for all those looking for that nudge to get started … and to get on with life through play."

David Kincaid, Founder, Managing Partner, LEVEL5 Strategy Inc.

"To know Janet Omstead is to know someone who appreciates living … and living life to the fullest. Janet has always brought enthusiasm and common sense to day-to-day life. This book reflects her approach to making the challenges of life fun, energetic, and worthwhile. To read Janet Omstead is to get a brief glimpse into what makes her tick, and helps make us all live life to the fullest. Reading *The Play Book* will put a smile on your face, a sparkle in your eye, a spring in your step, and challenge you to want to feel better. After all, beginning with a healthy, open mind is surely a great start to a healthy life. Play on!"

John Shannon, Broadcaster

"Janet captures the very essence of creating an active and healthy lifestyle that fosters improved well-being to ultimately increase confidence as well as joy in who we are and the journey we are on. This is a great read to get you fired up, with easy-to-implement strategies for improved health and a positive mindset."

Paula Simpson Morand, CEO, Brand You Studio

The Play Book

HOW TO GET IN THE HABIT OF GOOD HEALTH

Daniela!
Keep playing!
xox Janet

JO JANET OMSTEAD

JO JANET OMSTEAD

Text copyright © Janet Omstead, 2019. Rereleased 2023.

All rights reserved. No part of this publication may be reproduced, stored in a retrieval system or transmitted, in any form or by any means, without prior written consent of the publisher.

Disclaimer: All content in this book has been created and published for informational purposes only. It is not intended to be a substitute for professional medical advice and should not be relied upon as health or personal advice. Always seek the guidance of your doctor or other qualified health professional with any questions you may have regarding your health. Never disregard the advice of a medical professional, or delay in seeking it, because of something you have read in this book. Mention of specific companies, organizations, or authorities in this book does not imply endorsement by the publisher, nor does mention of specific companies, organizations, or authorities imply that they endorse this book. This book is presented solely for educational and entertainment purposes. Efforts have been made to ensure information is correct and accurate. Internet addresses given in this book were accurate at the time it went to press.

ISBN 978-1-9991725-4-1 (paperback)
ISBN 978-1-9991725-3-4 (ebook)
ISBN 978-1-9991725-2-7 (audiobook)

Published by Janet Omstead
Printed in Canada

To order books, go to **www.janetomstead.com**
For marketing and publicity inquiries, please contact **info@janetomstead.com**

Book producer: Tracy Bordian/AtLargeEditorial.com
Editors: Tracy Bordian, Eleanor Gasparik, and Wendy Thomas
Cover and interior design: Tracy Bordian and Rob Scanlan/First Image
Page layout: Rob Scanlan/First Image
Illustrations: Christopher Rouleau
Index: Wendy Thomas

For all those who have helped me on my play journey:

My parents, Jack and Anne, the reasons I exist in the first place — for laying the foundation for my love of play in the outdoors, adventure, and travel, especially YMCA Geneva Park and Whistler

My circle of friends and family — who inspire me and find a way to play, sing, and dance when we spend time together

My life loves — Meredith and Jack, the greatest playmates I could ever wish for — and my dog Cooper, too!

My life partner and soulmate, Shawn (Omer) — whose unwavering love and support plays on through all of life's ups and downs and for whom I am eternally grateful

CONTENTS

FOREWORD

by Adam Growe

I live a healthy lifestyle. In fact, I love being active — hockey, basketball, and running are my "hobbies" — but that doesn't mean I get in the recommended 20 minutes of activity every day. So if I already enjoy exercise and know that I *should* be doing something every day, why *aren't* I?

In *The Play Book*, Janet Omstead shows us how to get into the habit of good health by playing a little every day. And while Janet isn't the first fitness expert to promote the importance of daily activity, her fun, practical, and realistic approach makes it easier to infuse daily play into our lives so that exercise doesn't feel like a boring or monotonous regime.

Every chapter in *The Play Book* is energized by Janet's ability to put a positive lens on living an active lifestyle with joy. This is important. It's just not practical for me to play hockey, basketball, or even run every day. In fact, I won't be able to participate in those sports forever. If I don't make other types of exercise fun ... well, I won't do them.

Janet helps crack that nut.

She starts by effectively introducing the notion of letting our personal values guide our actions, and then takes our appreciation of putting play into our daily movement to another level. In addition, through personal interviews with six active living experts, including a specialist in neuropsychiatry, Janet explains the "brain–play" connection.

Understanding the importance of movement to our physiology and psychology — no matter the type of activities you enjoy or the physical limitations you live with — is a powerful motivator.

With Janet's help you will "see the world as a place that is full of opportunities to chase health and wellness through play." You'll learn how to look at the world around you and see that "functional movement spaces are everywhere": a set of stairs, your office, the garden, a parking lot, a kitchen counter, an elevator... You'll be equipped with powerful strategies to help you overcome obstacles that may be preventing you from moving more or sustaining any activity that you already like to do.

As you read the pages of this book, your immediate takeaway will be to feel more inclined to "do fewer things that suck." In the months after you read this book, you can take advantage of the resources Janet provides to help deconstruct the barriers in your life that may be keeping you on the sidelines. You will be empowered to live in a state of play.

Preface to this Reissued Edition

Sometimes I feel like Al Gore in his efforts to wake people up about climate change. I say it all the time: Like the climate crisis, the inactivity crisis is already here, but each of us can still act and make a change before it's too late.

Shortly after I launched *The Play Book* in 2019, the COVID-19 pandemic rocked all our lives. As the pandemic spread across the world, life as we knew it was cancelled. The pandemic wasn't a curve ball, it was a meteoroid! The global protective measures instilled by governments, from lockdowns to quarantining and social distancing, led to further physical inactivity, social isolation, worsening mental health, and increased chronic disease.

You'd probably agree that the pandemic gave us perspective on what's important and what truly matters — good health (physical and mental) and the quality of our relationships with family, friends, coworkers, and neighbours — and reminded us that life is short.

The pandemic brought to light how much our health depends on a daily investment in ourselves, from how we move, eat, sleep, and manage stress to the fundamental value of human connection, not to mention joy.

What was the outcome for those who didn't invest in their health, especially through play, before the pandemic? A 2021 study (published in the *British Journal of Sports Medicine*) of 48,440 adult patients in California found that if you were consistently inactive during the two years before COVID-19, the likelihood of hospitalization, admission to intensive care units, or death (compared to patients who regularly met physical activity guidelines) increased two and a half times. Besides age, pregnancy, and having an organ transplant, being sedentary was linked to the *highest* chance of being hospitalized with the coronavirus.

With the COVID-19 pandemic arguably behind us, have we as a society learned anything about taking care of our health? Believe it or not, despite all the best intentions by the fitness industry, policymakers, and institutions such as The World Health Organization (WHO), there has been no change in global inactivity levels since 2001.

So whose job is motivating people to move more and sit less? Is it the government, policymakers, and school boards' responsibility?

No.

The responsibility is squarely on our own shoulders. Putting someone else in charge of our health problems — whether a general practitioner, trainer, dietitian, social media "guru," partner, friend, or even a parent — is a recipe for failure. *The only way we can truly change is to choose to do something different.* The solution is reframing exercise as play and empowering ouselves to find what works for us, individually.

In her June 24, 2022, *Forbes Health* article, writer Sarah Hayes Coomer explains: "Prescribed plans fall apart because they don't account for the reality of your life: who you are, what you care about and how you spend your time. The way to get different results, of course, is to establish different behaviour patterns. The way to do that is to build a plan specifically for you—and by you—with your circumstances and priorities front and center. That's where a trained, certified master health coach comes in."

Since the COVID-19 pandemic began, I've been even more committed to my mission to end the inactivity crisis by inspiring the world to play for better health. And if you are reading this book, you have taken an important step in the right direction, arming yourself with the tools you need to help you achieve better health. Everything I originally wrote about health, well-being, and forming habits is more important than ever.

You are the expert in your life, and I believe in people's capacity for change and the necessity for self-care. Playing is the ultimate form of that, in my opinion.

As a behaviour-change health coach, it's my job to hold each person I have the honour to work with in unconditional positive regard. My clients work through self-directed, lasting changes to their behaviour, which are aligned with their values, to promote their health and wellness, and enhance their well-being.

People make changes because they want to, not because they should. Not surprisingly, one of the biggest catalysts for change as we age is when life gives us a wake-up call. (A global pandemic, anyone?)

The domino effect of moving our bodies has a direct positive impact on our physical and mental well-being. It's the ultimate form of self-care. When your stress levels are at an all-time high, having a daily routine, especially a habit of play that includes time for yourself, is crucial for navigating life's ups and downs.

Play is a powerful tool, a powerful force for change, that can reconnect you to your inner child while helping you discover the best possible system that works for you. The secret to getting more joy in your life is to play, and the secret to playing more is to do something that brings you joy. At the core is loving yourself enough to be proactive about your health.

Play can and will reconnect you to life's magic.

It does not matter how slowly you go as long as you do not stop.

—Confucius

PLEASE
LOOK
AFTER
YOURSELF

This Is NOT an Exercise Book

Imagine that you are holding two bottles of pills, one in each hand. One is labeled PLAY and the other is labeled NO PLAY.

The PLAY bottle holds a cure-all capsule that will help you feel happier and younger, keep your memory sharp, improve your sleep, strengthen your heart and muscles, and preserve your mobility, not to mention stave off a host of diseases.

The NO PLAY pills increase depression, wreck your hormone levels and sleep patterns, weaken your heart and muscles, reduce your mobility, and attract disease like a moth to a flame.

You can only take one pill. Which do you choose?

Put in these terms, the choice seems pretty clear, doesn't it? While there is no one magic pill, there is a simple choice you can make that will not only significantly improve your life but that will help you thrive.

Let's play

Much of the population views exercise as a tremendous effort, the most loathsome of tasks. It's the first thing to get moved to the bottom of the "to-do" list.

I get it. The world is spinning fast and life is busy — the job, the housework, the kids, extended family — whatever it may be. It can be hard to feel like we have time or space for anything else. And wading through all the health and fitness information in the media can be intimidating, too. But what if it doesn't have to be that complicated?

I've been a personal trainer and health coach since 2001. I've trained countless clients, from as young as 7 years old through to the age of 87, helping them to not only exercise effectively but also to adopt behaviour changes that will help them succeed in the long term. Through years of continued education and certifications, I have filled my "toolbox" so I could understand the psychology behind why we all make certain choices when it comes to our health and the steps needed to change our habits, form new ones, and get better results.

Understanding how habits are formed, how they are hardwired into our behaviour, struck a real chord with me. The brain is our command centre, and if it's not on board, your body will not follow. If something like a new habit is scary, dangerous, or uncomfortable, the brain is programmed to retreat. It's how we've survived since the time of the Neanderthals.

So I got to thinking: What if I took all that I've learned and understand about one habit — exercise — and reframe it in its simplest form? To strip it down and present it the way I truly see it? In a way that anyone, regardless of confidence, fitness level, or social status, can do?

Play as exercise.

No, this isn't me trying to disguise a word or use a clever marketing ploy. And it's not about having washboard abs or being on the cover of a magazine. *It's about taking control of your life so that you can live fully.*

> **The question you should be asking isn't "What do I want?" or "What are my goals?" but "What would excite me?"**
> —Tim Ferris

It's commonly understood that *work* and *play* are two different things (and if they aren't, you're a truly fortunate person). You might also think that *exercise* and *play* are two different things. But I want to encourage you to reconsider that notion.

What if play were simply the freedom to move your body in any way that brings you joy, makes you sweat a little, and smile a lot? Some examples include getting outside and biking, hiking, jumping, hula-hooping, running, scootering, skateboarding, skiing, horseback riding, playing tag or twister or hide and seek with your friends ... the possibilities are endless.

Playing is an incredible opportunity to find joy in life and to engage our mind, body, and spirit in the relentless pursuit of happiness. And it's *free.*

Playing is also part of our biology. When we are children, play is an important part of our development and learning. It brings a sense of wonder and belonging. It's also as natural as sleeping and eating.

> **You will never change your life until you change something you do daily. The secret of your success is found in your daily routine.**
> —John C. Maxwell

While I don't think adults forget how to play, I do think it becomes less of a priority. As we get older, our world expands and so do our interests. We get busy. We become preoccupied with making money rather than making time for having fun.

Think about it: When was the last time you found joy through movement and got excited about it? A time when you really couldn't wait to get going? When was the last time you lost yourself in play?

You don't need a gym, fancy exercise equipment, or a lot of space. You also don't need to set aside a lot of extra time for it. You can integrate play into your everyday routine. In fact, I think your life depends on it.

Invest in your health and longevity

Once you develop a habit of play, your brain, heart, and muscles will grow. Does it matter? Well, yes, if you want to age with function and vitality.

We need to be able to do more than simply walk when we get older. We also need to lift, reach, and bend. (These are called functional movements, and we'll discuss them more in the chapter "Functional Play," starting on page 63.) The only way for us to maintain these abilities is by practice. We have to constantly prepare our bodies for all of these situations.

How do you see yourself aging? What basic activities are you assuming you'll be able to do? We are told again and again to save for retirement. No one can argue that logic — people are living longer and require more financial savings to fund their desired standard of living. When it comes to our health, we need to apply the very same logic. If we invest in our well-being consistently throughout our lives, our health will also most likely be there for us to enjoy a good quality of life as we age.

Heal thyself through play

Play isn't for children only — it's essential for all human potential. Simply stated, it's one of the few ways we can make sense of emotions, gain more energy, and feel more alive. It's also one of the best ways to reduce stress. If we don't move or play, we run the inherent risk of disease.

When I first started personal training, I was awesome at writing exercise prescriptions for my clients with all sorts of pictures, charts, and schedules — my filing cabinets and shelves were full of programs

Sticking with something for the long term is the true path to anything worthwhile.
—Leo Babauta

tailored to each person's abilities. I came up with all kinds of amazing plans based on what my clients said they wanted. I was proud of my creativity and the time I invested to make each one unique. How many of my clients do you think actually did them? Maybe 10%, or less.

I realized that even the best exercise program in the world wouldn't work unless a person is ready, willing, and able to do the work on their own. And it definitely wasn't going to work if it wasn't fun! If something is too time consuming, too restricting, or too challenging, people just won't stick to it.

I also realized that one of the most helpful things I can do for my clients is help them understand what is realistic for their lifestyle, considering their demands and their abilities. I now view myself as more of a guide or problem solver, helping people put a puzzle together. My job is to help you find a way to play, to move more, that meets the needs of your life.

Find the solution that works for you

My goal isn't to tell you how to get fit. I want to motivate you to find the right health solution for yourself. Every person on this planet is unique. I want to help you focus on the reasons why you play or not, and to help empower you to make the choices you are ready, willing, and able to do.

In this book I'll show you:

- Play can be anything you want it to be as long as it gets you up and moving a little bit each day
- How to develop a playful mindset
- How to find opportunities for play every day, even when life throws you curve balls
- How little time you need to devote to play every day (it's less than you think!)
- How to play so you minimize your risk for injury

I'll also provide loads of inspiration and some handy ideas from my favourite health experts in the process.

Before you know it, a year will have passed and you will look and feel like a different person. A person who has made themselves and their health a priority. A person who has more energy to do what they really want to do. A person who stands tall and proud of their accomplishments.

Maybe even a person who has the confidence to ask for the promotion they want or the courage to do a thing that scares them.

The key will be in forming new habits and changing the way you talk to yourself. You'll need to throw away the "should" and foster a "get to" attitude. It's not "I should play." It's "I get to play." Change is hard yet not impossible. By tapping into your values, motivation, mindset, self-compassion, and time, you can achieve better health. (We'll cover this in detail in the next chapter.) And it will be fun, I promise!

> **Play is always accompanied by a feeling of "YES, this is what I want to do right now."**
> — Dr. Gray

There are no rules in this book, just tools you can use to drive your own play agenda by starting where you are at and considering what you are willing to do consistently. Understand fully that your body will take time to adapt to the changes you impose on it. If you are doing a little bit better and a little bit more, you will be thrilled with your newfound habit of play. You'll be surprised how little time you need to devote to it. (We cover this in "Play for Life," starting on page 117.)

The good news? It's never too late to rediscover your love for play. The great news? You don't need to be athletic.

One step at a time

One part at a time, one day at a time, we can accomplish any goal we set for ourselves.

—Karen Casey

HEAD
AND
BODY
INVESTED
TOGETHER

The Value in Play

Nothing frustrates me more than the New Year's resolution to "get in shape" and the crowded fitness centres filled with people who have a "now or never" or "all or nothing" mindset! They go too fast, too intensely, injure themselves, and then end up back on the couch, worse off than when they started.

The "30-day solution" plans drive me crazy, too. What happens when the 30 days are over? Have you learned how to exercise in a way that builds your body up rather than breaks it down? Have you learned healthy habits that you can sustain? Have you learned how to manage your exercise when you are travelling or when life gets in the way?

My bet is that the answer is a resounding "no."

The truth is that most people abandon their resolutions by January 17. That's 17 days! *Whaat!?*

Instead of an all-or-nothing approach, how about developing an attitude toward play that incorporates movement into your day, month, and year … for life?

Business coach, writer, and speaker Achim Nowak wrote a terrific article called "When We Hit Play." In it Nowak suggests we "make play a conscious value." He explains,

> The moment I decide that a sense of play matters, opportunity for playful engagement shout at me from every corner. It's a choice.

I agree wholeheartedly. It is imperative that we see the world as a place that is full of opportunities to chase health and wellness through play rather than a chance to sit on the sidelines.

It really doesn't have to be hard or complicated. Let's use a day at the office as an example. Think of a time in your day where you can add more movement, more play. Can you use the stairs? Take two at a time! Waiting for the bus? Stand on one leg! Set a timer to remind yourself to intentionally stand up every 30 to 45 minutes for 1 minute. Taking a coffee break? Go the long way! Parking the car? Park a little bit further away. Having a meeting on a nice day? Take it outside and walk while you talk.

Moving a bit more every day can lead to better sleep, a sunnier disposition, more energy, reduced stress, happier relationships, and a renewed sense of fun!

Make the decision to change

When you consider your state of health, are you thriving or merely surviving? Do you feel stressed all the time? Isolated? Burnout and depression affected all age groups throughout the pandemic. It's easy to ignore your health. As a result, people don't do anything at all. They are simply too exhausted to think about how unhealthy they are.

If you haven't been able to make your health a priority, I could certainly tell you why I think you need to make a change. But is that really going to motivate you to actually make a change? Probably not.

It can be very hard to know where to start when you have found more barriers than reasons to begin.

I see this happen a lot when I'm coaching people. My client might not feel as capable of making a change on their own as they originally thought. What I want for them and what they might be able to do aren't necessarily the same thing. They just aren't ready to embrace change.

> **Health is the crown on the well man's head that only the ill man can see.**
> —Robin Sharma

For example, one of my clients wants to drink less alcohol. They would like to do something about changing their habit (because they hear that drinking is dangerous to their health), but they just can't seem to change their behaviour. Why? When they drink wine they love how it tastes, they enjoy their meal more, it makes them social, and it even gives them extra time at the dinner table with their family.

They value the joy of drinking wine over the risks it poses to their health. The idea of stopping (or starting) a habit can feel overwhelming.

They want to change but they don't. Does this sound familiar? Every person I meet or work with feels like this about *something*. Eating fewer carbs, exercising, hitting the "right" number on the scale, drinking, sleeping, etc.

In her Ted Talk called "How to Make Hard Choices," philosopher Ruth Chang says that when it comes to making hard choices, each of us has the power to create our own reasons to either do or not do something. Ultimately the choices we end up making are influenced by the things we value.

I think this notion about values is really important. When you understand what you value and what you don't, it's a whole lot easier to navigate choices. You just need to ask yourself which choice better aligns with your beliefs and values. So instead of me telling you what I think you should do, let me ask you this: When it comes to your mobility, independence, and freedom, what kind of future do you hope for yourself?

Change is possible, but it must start with self-acceptance.
—Alexander Lowen

IDENTIFY YOUR CORE VALUES

When you understand who you are and where you are going, it's easier to decide the path you want to take. I've provided self-assessments on pages 149 to 151 to help you identify your personal values.

Get into the habit of taking care of yourself

Since you were born, you have learned how to function simply through habits you developed in daily life. The habits that help support life — what time you wake up, brush your teeth, get dressed, eat breakfast, go to work/school, have lunch, go home, get groceries, make/eat dinner, do chores, have a bath, go to sleep — aren't difficult, but they all needed to be practiced before they came naturally.

Let's face it, we've all been in the habit of performing certain "routines" or "tasks" for years. We settle into these patterns, often mindlessly, until one day they aren't working for us so much anymore or something happens that forces us to break a habit (getting sick, for example).

Getting into the habit of taking care of ourselves can seem daunting. But we already have the tools to be successful inside ourselves. We just need to peel the layers back — like an onion — to reveal how we can work with our personality tendencies rather than fight them.

REMEMBER HOW YOU USED TO PLAY

Identifying how you liked to play when you were young will help to shape your path to success. Complete the self-assessment on pages 152 to 153 to reveal the fun you can still find and how you might play a little more.

Keep it simple

Fitting play into an already busy life is difficult for many of us. Developing a strategy where you *can* find the time to play is part of a playful mindset.

If you keep your play strategy simple enough and small enough, odds are better that you'll return to it tomorrow, and the days after, until you develop a habit of play.

Take the stairs

Leo Babuta, author of *The Power of Less: The Fine Art of Limiting Yourself to the Essential … in Business and in Life,* has a philosophy that might help you make the task easier: Less is more. Leo says,

> Choose something so small that success is almost guaranteed. Sure, a small success is not as satisfying as a big success, but it's only small in the short term. If you start out with a small success, you can build upon it, get another small success, and build upon that, and so on — until you have a series of small successes that add up to a very large success. And that's much better than a large failure.

You really don't have to "work-out" for hours a day. Start small. You'll enjoy yourself more if you set achievable goals that work for your schedule. What to do and how much time to set aside for it are completely up to you. Just experiment until you find what suits you best. If it's easy, ridiculously easy for you to do,

> **Focus is the most important factor in determining whether you'll achieve a goal or stick to creating a new habit.… If you can maintain your focus on a goal or habit, you will more often than not achieve that goal or create that habit.**
>
> —Leo Babatua

chances are you are more likely to love it, stay with it, and be successful at it. Here's how you can start to shift your thinking:

1. **Focus on one thing.** It can be as simple as walking (but, heck, it can be anything that is movement based). Make this something you can try every day for a week … then a month … then a year!

2. **Keep it simple.** It needs to be something you know you can do 100% every day. Don't fall into the trap of biting off more than you can chew because you are super keen (for example, run a marathon without training — you would just hurt yourself). Simple steps to progress. That is all!

3. **Do less than you think you can — that way you will always feel like you've succeeded.** Write it down and make it measurable.

4. **Pick the same time every day.** When you first wake up? After dinner? During lunch hour? (We discuss creating a personal time chart in the next chapter.) This is *how* a habit is born.

5. **Keep a journal so you can record every day you do your practice.** Remember: There is no failure. Sometimes you might not be able to play, and that's okay. Keep confident that you will be able to get back on track because of #2!

The more consistently you build on that simple habit the more likely it is to stick. And, according to James Clear, an author and expert on how to build good habits, "what matters most in the beginning is establishing a new normal and building a new routine that you will stick to; not the results that you get." Once your movement/play becomes automatic, it will start adding value to your health and longevity and begin to replace the idea that you need to rely on willpower to move more.

Although change is hard, small, consistent steps practiced daily will start the motivation ball rolling and will lead to success. And if you can't do it for yourself, do it for someone else. Put your oxygen mask on first before you help someone else. Move for someone else who can't. One of my biggest acts of love for my kids is taking care of myself first. Happy mom = happy life. If you need to, dedicate your play in honour of someone else.

Bottom line: If you pick something that makes you happy, something that already aligns with what you value in life, you are more likely to stick to it and reap the mental and physical benefits. You'll start to feel good.

Start where you are. Use what you have. Do what you can.
—Arthur Ashe

TRACK YOUR PLAY

Tracking your play is an important step in moving toward a habit of good health. Whether you show up every day or miss a couple of days, this is invaluable feedback for knowing if you picked the right activity. How can you reshape your "rules" so that it's super easy for you to succeed? Keep going until it's something you do every day. Use the play tracker at the back of the book (page 155) to keep accountable to yourself.

WHAT THE EXPERTS SAY

Dr. Krista Scott-Dixon, Ph.D.

Dr. Krista Scott-Dixon is a former university researcher and professor who escaped academia to pursue her passion for goofing around on the internet answering health and fitness questions. She runs the women's weight training website **stumptuous.com** and is the author of several books, including *Why Me Want Eat*, a workbook for people struggling with food and eating issues. After spending nearly 15 years creating coaching certification and education programs, she now works with a digital health app helping people change their nutrition behaviours. She also lectures and delivers training worldwide.

JO: Why do we need to be conscious of and actually plan for some daily exercise?

KS: I would argue that post–World War II there was a real shift away from an agricultural economy toward increasing mechanization, increasing industrialization, and suburban living, all of which more and more took people out of daily physical activity. Exercise has become less life based.

For example, my grandmother is 93. She walks every day, but I've observed her patterns of activity and she just does stuff, that's her exercise. She tried going to the gym once or twice, but she was like "this is boring"! She has a garden, and her housework, and she finds ways to do things. A lot of it is outside, and a lot of it is not exercise: she does something for half an hour and then has a little sit, and then does another thing for half an hour and has another sit. It's a very organic kind of thing.

I think we're increasingly understanding that the concept of exercising for function got lost along the way.

JO: Can we create a habit of exercise if our wellness depends upon it?

KS: Sure! We do lots of things we don't want to do, or that we aren't naturally inclined to do. The example I always use is *not pee in our pants*. Going to the bathroom is a biological function, and we all have to do it — sometimes we need to do it more urgently than other times. But, by and large, most of us have figured out the level of personal control required not to pee in our pants. I think humans can learn anything.

JO: How do we encourage people to be more active?

KS: Something we need to remember is that most people, especially adults, don't know what feeling good feels like anymore. If we are people who are active, we take care of our health, we believe in the power of play, we have a good social environment — we know what feeling good is like, right? We get up in the morning, feel good, and we are like, "Yeah, it's tennis time" or whatever it is we do. So we can access a mental model of feeling good in our head and we are like "Ooh, that is what I want. I know how to go and get that." But most adults, I would argue, have lost the mental model of feeling good, which kids just do intuitively. So part of helping people recapture that "feel good" model is re-teaching them what it feels like to be a kid and how to play in a very open-ended, unstructured, intrinsically enjoyable way.

JO: What should be the goal of exercising? And what can help people reach it?

KS: I think the goal should always be feeling better! So much of exercise now is feeling worse — *I'm going to finish a CrossFit workout and puke.* Why would I ever want to do that?! That sounds terrible.

What if we flipped the goal from achieving as much as possible today to a goal of always being able to show up tomorrow and do the exact same thing? It changes the game. If I want to show up tomorrow and walk my dog, what has to happen today? How do I have to structure that dog walk? Maybe I won't go on a three-hour dog run, but instead go around the block once or twice because I know I can show up and do that again tomorrow.

And organically, spontaneously, I'll want to do more — if it's effortless, effortless, effortless! If I've been taking my dog for a walk for 5 minutes, there is going to be a day when I'm like, "Goddammit, let's just do 10." That day is going to happen. I don't need to force it. Once they tap into that feeling, people generally want to do more and more and more, slowly raising their comfortable threshold.

JO: What is the BAM (bare-ass minimum) for people?

KS: It's WHATEVER IT IS FOR YOU! The bare-ass minimum is all about your own personal baseline that you are absolutely committed to do under *any* circumstances.

I like that model because most people start from 100 and work backward. They start with the perfect thing and work from there — being the perfect mom, or having the perfect body, or the perfect exercise. And that's a very insidious thought when you start from 100 and start subtracting — like I didn't do this, and I didn't do this, and here are all the ways I sucked! Starting from 0 and working upward is really, really important because it's constantly a win! And that is play!

JO: Why is movement important?

KS: We know that movement enhances learning, movement enhances cognition, movement enhances memory and mental health. We think with our bodies. There is a distinction between brain and body in terms of physical health, but the brain isn't separate. I would say that we have become unaccustomed to using our bodies to think with. We have been trained to ignore sensory input, to ignore kinetic input. We have been trained out of using our bodies as sensory organs and cognitive apparatuses.

When you see kids interact with new things, what do they do? They put it in their mouth, they manipulate it, they throw it, they test the weight — they hit their sister with it! They have a very movement- and sensory-based experience of the world. Over time we are taught — trained — that's not appropriate. You don't put things in your mouth! You don't touch things. You don't touch other people. People forget that they are allowed to do stuff. I think a lot of people don't even know what the options are! It's saying: "Hey, have you ever tried this!?" And our discovering, "I didn't know this was a thing" or "Oh … I can do that?" A lot of it is about exposure.

JO: What do you feel are the most important side effects of play?

KS: Increased happiness, joyfulness, increased connection to other people and to yourself, a sense of embodiment — being connected in your body, a greater sense of self-efficacy, competence.

JO: What is holding men and women back from the habit of play?

KS: I tend to look for structural reasons first, rather than individual reasons. Not that individual reasons aren't relevant, but I would argue that systemic structural and environmental factors are the biggest reasons. These shape our experience and shape our desires, behaviours, and thoughts in ways that we aren't aware of. A perfect example is the layout of a city. The healthiest cities are walkable, have bike paths and nature trails, have good weather and low pollution. It's not that those cities have better people in them; it's that they're designed around playing.

JO: What if we don't live in a city that encourages play?

KS: Maybe I cannot change my physical environment, but I should still think about and recognize how my environment affects things. Can I make my environment more conducive to play? How could I prioritize play in my environment? Are there possibilities open to me that I might not have recognized? I have a thought experiment I like: If I *had* to play, if someone put a gun to my head and said "You *have* to play," how would I figure that out?

Start with the fundamental premise that there are options you are not seeing — and now we make a game of it. How could you play? "Oh, hey, I have a kid, that kid has a baseball glove. We have a backyard. Awesome. Let's go throw the ball around." One of our coaches built a climbing wall in his basement. A friend of mine who lives in a one-bedroom apartment decided she was sitting on the couch and watching TV too much, so she got rid of her couch! So, what if it's not adding stuff but taking stuff away? What is standing in your way and making it way too easy to do unwanted things? It's about challenging people to come up with options.

TRY
INCREASING
MOVEMENT
EVERY DAY

Your Playful Heart

Improving your lifestyle through play can do wonders for your health, but you might worry that you aren't doing things "perfectly" — and that sucks the fun right out of the process. You want to bring joy into moving more (and feeling better) so focusing on perfection can defeat the purpose. It's not about how others are doing but about how *you* are doing and what works as *your* "play." Remember, we're talking about playing and moving for overall health rather than training and moving for a specific achievement, such as running a marathon.

You don't need an hour

Did you know that the only reason people think they need to work out for an hour is because that's how instructors and trainers bill for their time? Yup … it's true! Over time, the fitness industry has convinced everyone that the *only* way to get healthy is to join a gym and do lengthy workouts. This is so unfortunate because it means people are set up to fail. This failure leads to inactivity … and inactivity is literally killing people.

> **Doing something physical each day boosts brain function, fuels far higher energy levels, helps you manage stress more effectively, and keeps you in the game longer.**
> —Robin Sharma

In 2018, The American College of Cardiology reported that in the United States, "an estimated $117 billion in annual healthcare costs and about 10% of premature deaths are associated with inadequate physical activity. Although the latest federal monitoring data shows some improvements in physical activity levels among U.S. adults (2016), and adolescents (2015), only 26% of men, 19% of women, and 20% of adolescents report performing enough activity."

You don't have to be part of those statistics.

I'm tired of seeing people who want to be active and healthier not bother because it's too much effort and there is far too much conflicting information swirling in the media. What if I told you that you *can* live out the rest of your years, actively aging, maintaining independence, and never going on a diet again? And you *don't* have to join a gym?

The not-so-secret is this: It's about how all the movement you do in a day — 5 minutes here, 10 minutes there — adds up. It's the *cumulative effect* of movement.

And the best news: All kinds of movement can help you achieve your goal, not just time spent in a gym. In Dan Buetner's bestselling book *The Blue Zones,* he discusses the areas of the world where people live the longest. Did you know that the people who have lived the longest have never set foot in a gym?

So you really *do* have the time. You *can* make it happen. You just have to break through the stigma that anything less than an hour isn't good enough.

What are the costs of not playing?

All around us we see the effects of living in an industrialized world: people are playing less, eating more, relying on pharmaceutical opioids to relieve pain, working longer hours, spending more time commuting, and sitting more. Physical inactivity is now recognized as one of the leading global risk factors for morbidity and premature mortality. But the good news is that people benefit from even *modest* activity. In a study where individuals who were active, even at levels less than recommended (about 2.5 hours per week), lived 3 years longer than inactive individuals. Being active just 10% more could account for 533,000 fewer deaths a year *worldwide.* A 25% increase in activity could prevent 1.3 million deaths. Whoa! If we wiped out inactivity altogether, life expectancy would increase to a degree comparable to doing away with smoking or obesity.

Many diseases are preventable. Just by moving more and practicing functional movements that mimic everyday life, you can prevent diseases and conditions such as high blood pressure, Type 2 diabetes, and a host of cancers — and that means you can potentially live longer!

Several studies express their findings this way: “One study found that the recommended 150 minutes of weekly activity makes you 31% less likely to die over a 14-year period.” What does “less likely to die” mean? It means “you will live longer.” And why does increased activity lead to better health? In a significant study done on highly active male and female cyclists aged 55 to 79, scientists found that the cyclists' T-cells, which help to control infection, were stronger than those in individuals who were not active, and further concluded that the cyclists had the immune systems of a 20-year-old. This is just one of many examples of why movement can increase life expectancy.

What is your BAM?

BAM is a term I learned when I began my coaching journey, and I loved the idea so much that I share it with clients who don't feel that they can squeeze another minute to “workout” into their day. It stands for “bare-ass minimum” and it refers to the least amount of movement you are willing to start with each day, an amount of time you are 100% sure you can commit, to begin to make a positive impact on your health. That doesn't sound so bad, does it?

> **The choice to play is up to you as well as how you go about it.**
> —Dr. Peter Gray

The World Health Organization recommends 150 minutes of aerobic or cardio (heart-pumping) activity *a week* at a variety of intensities where you still have the ability to talk while in motion but you're not panting or unable to speak. Canada's Physical Activity Guide for Healthy Active Living recommends 4 to 7 sessions a week of this type of exercise for more than 20 minutes per session, depending on your level of experience and intensity. (Check out The Canadian Society for Exercise Physiology [**csep.ca**] for physical activity guidelines for all age groups.)

Don't have 20 minutes? What about 10 minutes two times a day? Or break it down further: how about 5 minutes four times a day? You get the idea.

A number of exceptionally diverse and educated experts all agree it's time to look at the whole day as an opportunity to move more and sit less. Introducing even 1 more minute of activity to your daily schedule might not seem like much, but as you begin to enjoy the benefits, you'll likely add more. It's a lot like the concept of compounded interest. A little consistent investment over time pays off big gains in the long run, even if it's just 1% better every day. In his latest book *Atomic Habits,* James Clear speaks to this concept: "Habits are the compound interest of self-improvement. The same way that money multiplies through compound interest, the effects of your habits multiply as you repeat them. They seem to make little difference on any given day and yet the impact they deliver over the months and years can be enormous."

Is there a minimum play investment you might want to consider for a healthier future? Can you see how bare-ass minimums can really be a way to kick-ass maximums?

Let's do some math (this is good for me as I'm not a math girl — but I can use a calculator):

- 24 hours in a day (*everyone* gets these!)
- You sleep 8 hours (hopefully) a day.
- You are awake 16 hours. That gives you 960 (16 × 60) minutes a day to work with. The recommended amount of physical activity a week is 150 minutes, so:
  150 ÷ 7 (7 days in a week) = 21.42 minutes a day
  Let's round that up to 22 minutes a day.

Can you find 22 minutes in the 960 minutes you have in a day? Still too much? Well, you know, you don't have to do those 22 minutes all at once. The effect continues as we leapfrog through to the target 22 minutes a day:

- 5 minutes of movement 4.4 times
- 8 minutes of movement 2.75 times
- 11 minutes of movement 2 times
- 15 minutes of movement 1.46 times
- 20 minutes of movement 1.1 times
- 22 minutes of movement 1 time!

Consider the build up from 1 minute to 22 minutes a day as a slow, steady process. Don't rush yourself. Take a year, or longer. For example, if you start at 5 minutes per day and add 1 minute per day each month, at the end of year you'd be at 17 minutes a day. Highly commendable! And the pace of increase gives you a month to get used to each new level.

Even if you can't meet your BAM, the bottom line is that if we make movement playful — fun — it will be something you love enough to still be doing 20 years from now. As Abraham Lincoln famously said, "In the end, It's not the years in your life that count, it's the life in your years." Let's get more out of life!

Do your heart good

What kind of movement will help you reach your BAM? Start with anything that makes you get a little sweat on — brisk walking, taking stairs, horsing around with your children and/or pet, riding a bike. All of these count toward your goal of 22 minutes of play per day.

When choosing activities, try to include cardio exercises. These heart-pumping movements cause your body to release endorphins naturally — endorphins are your happy and pain-killing hormones — and also improve your circulation because more oxygen is going into your blood. Increasing oxygen decreases stress.

Determining Your Target Heart Rate Zone

To be considered exercise, I don't believe an activity "should be" a mountain that is hard to climb. Rather, it can be part of something you like to do every day — whether that's dancing, walking, or picking up your grandkids! Aaron E. Carrol, a professor at Indiana University School of Medicine, said it well: "Moderate intensity is probably much less than you think. Walking briskly, at 3 to 4 miles per hour or so, qualifies. So does bicycling slower than 10 miles an hour. Anything that gets your heart rate somewhere between 110 and 140 beats per minute is enough. Even vacuuming, mowing the lawn, or walking your dog might qualify."

Those who do not move, do not notice their chains.
—Rosa Luxemburg

So how fast is 110 to 140 beats per minute? Use this simple calculation to find your personal target heart rate: subtract your age from 220. Let's use me as an example: 220 – 51 = 169. So 169 is my maximum heart rate, which means if I reach that number, it's most likely difficult for me to keep it up — I will have a hard time breathing/exchanging oxygen and talking.

Using heart rate as my guide, I can determine various intensity levels and the value each has on my health. Here is what the ranges of beats per minute equate to (for ease of reference, I've rounded them up):

<table>
<tr><th></th><th>Heart Rate</th><th>Exertion</th><th>Feels</th><th>Value</th></tr>
<tr><td></td><td>85–101</td><td>50–60%</td><td>Very easy</td><td>Enhances general health; assists recovery</td></tr>
<tr><td rowspan="3">Improves Fitness</td><td>101–118</td><td>60–70%</td><td>Easy</td><td>Increases endurance; fat-burning zone</td></tr>
<tr><td>118–135</td><td>70–80%</td><td>Reasonable</td><td>Expands aerobic health</td></tr>
<tr><td>135–152</td><td>80–90%</td><td>Hard</td><td>Builds up max performance ability</td></tr>
<tr><td></td><td>152–169</td><td>90–100%</td><td>Very hard</td><td>Magnifies max performance and speed</td></tr>
</table>

Obviously, working at the very easy level is going to be the first step. Jumping in to the most challenging level is a mistake if you haven't moved your body very much. (Wouldn't want to send your heart into shock — death is what we're trying to avoid with all this playing around!)

HOW TO TRACK YOUR HEART RATE

Now, there are also downloadable apps for smartphones and watches that have built-in heart rate trackers. It's a personal choice whether you want to use an app, but quite frankly, tracking in real time how your heart is responding to the stress you are putting on it is valuable feedback. Knowing your heart rate allows you to understand how hard your heart is working in comparison to how you feel. Many of my clients are surprised that they are often not working hard enough to attain the value they're trying to achieve. Regularly checking their heart rate keeps them accountable to themselves when they are playing! I have a number of heart rate monitors that I lend out for a couple of weeks just to get my clients started.

That said, tracking your heart rate with a fancy watch isn't for everyone. The good-enough version is to take a measurement by finding your pulse along your neck. Place your index and middle finger on your neck near the carotid artery (that's the big artery just to the side of your throat or windpipe below your jaw line). When you feel your heart beat, look at the second hand on a watch. It's best to then pause during play and count the number of pulses you feel for 10 seconds. Whatever that number is, multiply it by 6 to get your heart beats per minute. YouTube has a number of videos on "How to check your pulse on your neck" that demonstrate this technique.

Your time-out line

Every person on the planet has the same gift of time: 24 hours every day. Only you can decide how to use, or waste, those hours. In Chapter 2 you went through the process of determining what kinds of activities you value most. Now you need to start thinking about how you can combine the activities you value most with the time you have to enjoy them.

Here's another way to think about it: During a football game players typically get 4 time-outs. What if you treated your day like a game where you give yourself 4 time-outs? Like any good coach, you want to make sure you use those time-outs to regroup, strategize, and execute your game plan. The best coaches in the world use all of their time-outs. Use 2, 3, 4 — as many as you want to meet your activity goals.

Having routines/systems can super-charge your day while simultaneously creating a sense of calm and sanity in your life. When people can't find the time in their busy lives for increasing their movement, I suggest they create a "time-out" line. It's a way to understand the different tasks that take up our time and to see if there are places to carve out some minutes to move a little more. (Fun fact, scheduling less time to complete your play task forces your brain to focus.)

Here's how it works: Take out a regular lined sheet of paper. Down the left-hand column write out the hours in 30-minute increments from 5 a.m. to 10:30 p.m. Pick a day of the week to record *everything* you do from when you first wake up to when you go to bed. (On page 44 I have included a sample of one of my days showing the when, what, and where of my activities.) The next day, look at the data. How much time did you spend eating, in transit, in meetings, surfing the internet, scrolling through social media, working at your desk, running errands, etc. Where could you find windows to play? And what would be the typical starting/minimum amount of time you can spend building a play habit? What is realistic and easiest for you?

Because this is your own unique blueprint, I suggest you start with your bare-ass minimum — the place where you can be sure you will succeed 100% of the time. I have clients who start with 1 minute and others who start with 5 minutes. Consistency is key, and so is fun!

Can you get up 5 minutes earlier and do some stretches? Could you take a 5-minute walk after dinner? How about doing chair squats while you brush your teeth? What about a few minutes of gentle yoga before you fall asleep?

Working with your "time-out line," see if you can identify the activity that can serve as the cue for carrying out your chosen exercise (like returning to your desk and doing squats before sitting down). There is no right or wrong choice. The key is to pick a habit that's enjoyable, focus on it consistently, and keep practising. Start small! Over time, as you see the fun in this type of play and as you find what works for you, increase the time every couple of weeks.

Some people like to print off the habit tracker, like in Chapter 2, and post it somewhere — like a bathroom mirror — and check off the days they are able to do the new "play" routine. This type of feedback will give you a boost to carry on or tell you that it's not working for you — at that point, you can choose something different that will be a better fit.

> People who seem to stick to good habits with ease are often benefitting from an environment that makes those behaviours easier.
> —James Clear

Sample: My Time-out Line for a Monday

Time	Activity	Position
5:00 a.m.	Sleep	Lying down
5:30 a.m.	Sleep	Lying down
6:00 a.m.	Wake up	Standing
6:30 a.m.	Run with husband	Standing
7:00 a.m.	Catch up on e-mails	Standing
7:30 a.m.	1st client	Standing
8:00 a.m.	Bank	Standing
8:30 a.m.	Breakfast	Seated
9:00 a.m.	Walk dog with my friend	Standing
9:30 a.m.	Walk dog with my friend	
10:00 a.m.	Stretch and set agenda for the day	Seated
10:30 a.m.	Write book	Seated
11:00 a.m.	Write book	Standing
11:30 a.m.	Write book	Standing
12:00 p.m.	Write book	Seated
12:30pm	Lunch	Seated
1:00 p.m.	Lunch	Standing
1:30 p.m.	Client prep	Seated
2:00 p.m.	Zoom meeting	Standing
2:30 p.m.	Zoom meeting	Seated

3:00 p.m.	Client calls	Standing
3:30 p.m.	Client calls	Standing
4:00 p.m.	Finish client prep	Seated
4:30 p.m.	Grocery store	Standing
5:00 p.m.	Start dinner prep	Standing
5:30 p.m.	Dinner prep	Standing
6:00 p.m.	Eat dinner	Seated
6:30 p.m.	Leave for choir	Subway
7:00 p.m.	Choir	Seated/standing
7:30 p.m.	Choir	
8:00 p.m.	Choir	
8:30 p.m.	Choir	
9:00 p.m.	Home from choir	Subway
9:30 p.m.	Ready for bed	Standing
10:00 p.m.	Bed	Lie down!
10:30 p.m.	Sleep	

FIND YOUR TIME-OUT

See page 156 for a template you can use to create your own “time-out line.”

When you're assessing your typical day, you might think there's just no room for anything else — everything you already do has a purpose and needs to be done. That's why spending time looking at your days — and looking for windows of play opportunity — is so important: We might not immediately make a connection between the patterns and steps we routinely take day after day and the way we function. What do you do out of habit? And is it time to change that habit?

Everyone I've coached struggles with change. But often change is not as hard — and to be honest, as fast — as some make it out to be. It's an evolving process. Skills, like exercise, when broken into bite-size pieces, are easy to take on and develop. Inserting a play habit before you do a current ritual is a convenient place to start.

WHEN IS YOUR ENERGY AT ITS BEST?

Are you a low-energy morning person? Don't plan to do 5 jumping jacks when you fall out of bed! A high-energy after-morning-coffee person? Walk around your yard, house, block, or office building. Ideally you want to try to schedule your play time when your energy is at its highest because that's when you will succeed.

Focus on one task

Stripping your play activity down to the simplest task and focusing only on accomplishing that one task is the best way you can makes it something you can stick with for life. For example, if your activity is a 5-minute walk in the morning, put your play clothes out the night before so that when you wake up you can automatically put them on and head out. We're not talking about quick results here (besides, they never stick!). We're talking about a plan that works for you day in and day out, with results that not only start but also keep coming. Remember: First and foremost, tackle something that's easy and achievable.

To become healthier as individuals and as a society, we need to become people who try different things, listen to our bodies, and find positive lifestyle changes that we can stick with for the long haul. There's no such thing as a one-size-fits-all solution when we look at health and fitness options. There's only what works for us as individuals. Once you've completed your time-out line you will see windows of opportunity where you get to play! After studying their time-out line, my clients are often surprised to discover that they move way less than they think they do. How aware are you of how much you currently move in a typical day?

WHEN WILL YOU PLAY?

- ❑ Immediately after getting out of bed
- ❑ Prior to eating breakfast
- ❑ After eating breakfast
- ❑ On the way to work
- ❑ During a morning break
- ❑ Prior to lunch
- ❑ During your lunch hour
- ❑ Right after lunch
- ❑ During an afternoon break
- ❑ Just as you leave work
- ❑ As part of your return trip home
- ❑ Prior to dinner
- ❑ After your last meal of the day
- ❑ Right before bedtime

HOW TO BEGIN AN ACTIVITY

1. Pick one type of movement.
2. Make it easy.
3. Make it easier.
4. Make it ridiculously, almost laughably, easy.
5. NOW start doing it.

When you think about your own reality, ability, and current patterns, what small action could you take *right now* to move you closer to your own play routine? Remember: it's not about being perfect, it's about getting better.

Shape your environment

By creating an environment in your home or office that supports your efforts to move more, you can start to pave the way to success. The aim is to build your internal motivation. How do you do that? Here are some ideas:

- Are you a morning person? Can you set your alarm 5 minutes earlier, roll out of bed onto the floor, and do some gentle stretching?

- Do you commute to work by public transportation? Could you stand rather than sit on the train or bus?
- Buy a pair of great running shoes and leave them beside your bed at night so you can put them on and get going in the morning.
- Are you leading a two-person or three-person business meeting? Could you move it into a walk in the park instead of a sit-in at the boardroom table?

Finding creative ways to shape your environment is like adding a silent partner to support your playtime. It means you're not totally reliant on your willpower, and that makes it easier on you to keep moving forward.

PACE YOURSELF

One of the biggest mistakes many people make is that they get super keen and try to do everything all at once. While I'm happy that you feel keen, please pace yourself so that you don't get injured, especially if it's been a while since you have been exercising regularly. Too much play can become a problem if you increase things too quickly. A good guideline is the 10% rule: no more than a

10% increase in frequency, duration, or intensity of play per week. For example, if you are committing to 10 minutes of walking, this week, using the 10% guideline, you can add a minute more next week. This way you are building up slowly and injury-free. By adding a minute every week, in just a short time you will be at 20 minutes!

Play smarter, not harder

The power lies within you to find workable strategies to exercise smarter and improve your health for good. You can begin listing them right now using a simple system appropriately called SMART goals. Corporations, schools, and organizations have used the SMART strategy to identify a direction toward a specific task or goal.

SPECIFIC
MEASURABLE
ACHIEVABLE
REALISTIC
TIME FRAME

When I interviewed the renowned Dr. Paul Oh, Medical Director of the Cardiovascular Prevention and Rehabilitation Program and Scientist at The Toronto Rehabilitation Institute, for this book, we built on the SMART acronym to encompass the play idea — and SMARTER was born!

SPECIFIC
MEASURABLE
ACHIEVABLE
REALISTIC
TIME FRAME
ENJOYABLE
REPEATABLE

Some clients I work with are used to setting personal goals, but others aren't. If a goal is too unreachable or is intangible, you likely won't go after it. An example would be flying to the moon if you've never even been in a spaceship. Not impossible, just not realistic. We all instinctively know that we need goals to achieve success. However, we still don't set them or write them down. Why? As author James Clear says, "Goals are good for setting a direction, but systems (habits) are best for making progress."

At a young age, we didn't know learning to walk was a goal, yet we all kept trying as we practised over and over and over until we were able to do it. We may not have written down walking as a goal, but we knew that accomplishing it meant a progression to running, jumping, skipping, hopping … wow!

That's why the result of a specific goal needs to be measurable, realistic, and repeatable and have a time frame, but more than that, *it must be enjoyable.*

Let's say your goal is walking more. That's a pretty broad statement. How can we break that down as a SMARTER goal?

Specific	Walk more
Measureable	To the stop sign and back
Achievable	Yes
Realistic	Yes
Time frame	2 weeks to accomplish
Enjoyable	Yes
Repeatable	Absolutely

Remember to pick an activity that you love to do and have fun.

Keep it simple

ALL-IN/ALL-OUT THINKING

Being able to stick with a plan that you've designed and can feel good about is very empowering. But sometimes things go off the rails. Have you ever decided to run a 5K and started training, and although things went well for a while, you quit? Maybe your expectations were unrealistic or life got in the way. Because you weren't successful you might think, "Well, I won't do anything at all because I've failed." Do you start something on a Monday, like a new exercise regime, and by Wednesday miss a day, so you think, "I can't even do three days in a row so I'm going to stop"? Have you considered that your expectations are not aligning with your own reality?

This is called the "all-or-nothing" mindset — if you let yourself down, you just give up.

If you miss a day of play, don't throw in the towel. Be aware of why you missed it and move on. Perhaps you were tired or sick. Or you scheduled something else in your allotted time. Maybe you were thinking that it's too hard so why bother? Everyone goes through this! Don't beat yourself up — forgive yourself.

If what you've chosen to do as play is too hard to do, fit in, or stick with, pick something easier. Choose something you're guaranteed to get done — aim for at least 8 out of 10 times achievable. Once you understand why you do what you do and get in the habit of following your own personal daily rituals, it *will* get easier!

Pick something easy

WHAT THE EXPERTS SAY

Dr. Paul Oh, MD, FRCPC

Dr. Oh is the GoodLife Fitness Chair in Cardiovascular Rehabilitation and Prevention, Medical Director of the Cardiovascular Prevention and Rehabilitation Program at Toronto Rehab, and a Senior Scientist at KITE. A leading expert on the role of exercise in rehabilitation, he leads a comprehensive research program that includes investigating best practices in cardiac rehabilitation and analyzing cardiovascular databases to better understand long-term patient outcomes.

JO: How would you summarize our current state of activity, or inactivity?

PO: On the surface, it would appear that Canadians are moderately active across the population. But when you look at it more closely, objectively measuring what people do on a regular basis, do they get 10,000 steps a day? Do they get 150 minutes of moderate to vigorous activity? Do they get 30 minutes in bouts of 10 minutes purposely, 5 to 7 days? The picture it paints is that 95% of Canadians just aren't doing enough.

We are starting from a place that some people might label as really "bad" and "dangerous." On the other hand, we are starting from a place of tremendous opportunity to do some simple things!

JO: And you're in the opportunity camp?

PO: Yes. Because when we look at the return on doing little bits of activity — using a graph to show the relationship between cardiovascular benefit and the amount of activity we do in minutes, or calories burned, or intensity — the steepest part of the curve is at the beginning. First steps are always the most important steps and give us the most benefit!

When people think about exercise, they go to the right end of the curve: Do I need to go run marathons? Do I need to be a triathlete? Do I have to put on fancy clothing, get sweaty, and fall down? That's not reachable — or even reasonable — for most of the population. Most of us are way back at the left side, much too sedentary and not really getting enough basic, moderate activity during the day.

JO: What does a moderate level of activity look like?

PO: It's really critical to reframe what we mean by moderate or "reasonable" exercise and physical activity. The simple and fundamental starting place is wherever you are. Just adding something — anything — is probably the most important first step. Ask yourself: Where am I right now and where can I be tomorrow?

Running for the gold is going to be a whole lot of pain, and it's not going to be enjoyable, and it's not going to be repeated. But going for a 5-minute walk, or going into the pool, or whatever it is that agrees with your own body and your own physiology, I think we need to find that.

So set the right kind of goal — a simple, "SMARTER" one — and find something that's enjoyable so you can actually get there in a small step. Then you have a small "win," can make that the habit, and then build from there.

JO: Can long-term goals be part of this?

PO: Absolutely, but reframing is important. For instance, a lot of folks will set weight loss as their goal, as the thing they really want. It may or may not come, so the challenge along the way is not to lose the enjoyment of all the things that you've done in a wonderful purposeful way toward that goal — going for a walk, eating something differently, thinking about something mindful. Those are all successes that may get swamped if we just focus on a scale and say, "If I didn't lose 10% of my bodyweight, it is a failure." Setting those short-term behavioural things that are SMARTER and fun means many successes throughout the process, which may lead to that long-term goal as well.

JO: What should be our measure of success?

PO: Don't let somebody else set the standard for you, let it be your own. It's wherever YOU are right now, where YOU want to be, and what's going to be YOUR first step. Success is just measured against your own levels of abilities, desires, wants.

JO: Does medication affect our abilities in the short or long term?

PO: Unfortunately, medications become a reality with many of the people that we see. It's a double-edged sword, right? Medicines can be life-saving but can also, for example, drag down your energy. But it's the whole package, coming to terms with the medicines in your life as well as all the other things [habits] that you are doing.

Medicines work better when you are active and being mindful of what you eat and what you do. I joke that the Aspirin will actually work better if you take it for a 30-minute walk every day!

Exercise can also help with managing some side effects of medications. If you have low energy, one way to get it back is actually getting up and moving about. There is good data that says 30 minutes of activity can be as powerful as any of the pills one takes. It can lower sugar as much as a diabetes pill; it can lower blood pressure as much as a blood pressure pill.

JO: What about mental health benefits?

PO: Exercise is a huge thing. Mental health, mood, memory in particular — we know exercise has terrific effects. Engaging in a good, structured physical activity exercise program can actually improve memory, executive function, our cognitive tasks, so it's a wonderful defence mechanism to help our brain function.

We also know that for depression and anxiety, exercise can absolutely help. We've seen the level of depression drop by about half in some people that we see! Just by doing some regular physical activity, like walking 30 minutes. Interestingly, some of our team have shown that resistance training [weight training] is particularly helpful for cognition, that there might actually be an interesting relationship between the amount of muscle tissue you have and how your brain works.

I would call physical activity a head-to-toe solution.

JO: What can motivate us to move more?

PO: For health behaviours, I think it's tough to be purely externally motivated, because that would depend a lot on other people. We need to get to where it's for us. This is something for me, by me, and I will find a way of getting enjoyment. So I think the play model is wonderful in this way because you actually get to internally motivate because it's fun, and I get a reward [health]. That's really what I want.

JO: But working in a group can be motivating as well for a lot of people?

PO: Absolutely. It's great because it goes in both directions: somebody might motivate you and you might motivate somebody else. So that's actually taking your internal and making it external for somebody else. I think that's a wonderful ultimate to get to. And that's why peer support works, that's why running groups work — because we feed off each other. But I still think you need to have your own purpose, be your own master, be autonomous in what you do, and then reach out and find your own connections.

JO: What do you see as key to upping our state of activity?

PO: Humans are designed to be successful when they can actually choose what they are doing [autonomy], learn whatever it is that they are doing, and get good at it! The notion of mastering. Think of the one-year-old that's just learning to walk, and when they get going, they don't stop. Some people have to relearn that when they are 50 years old, that we can actually walk again and it's great. And this applies to recognizing you can do things that you haven't done before. Those are wonderful kinds of discoveries.

FEEL

UNBELIEVABLY

NIMBLE

FUNctional Play

We all age, but each of us ages differently. Much of your aging process is based on genetic factors in your unique DNA. An article in *The Scientist Magazine* titled "How We Age" put it bluntly: "Growing old is a fact of life. And there's no mistaking it, given the increased fatigue, weakened bones, and ill health that generally accompany aging. Indeed age is the number one risk factor for a myriad of diseases, including Alzheimer's, cancer, cataracts, and macular degeneration."

Bummer.

Yet the quality of your aging process and your ability to prevent lifestyle-related diseases is more in your control than you think. Although a lot is happening naturally — memory loss, weakened bone density and cardiovascular system, hearing and vision loss, reduced skin elasticity, a receding gum line, sexual decline, and weight gain — you *can* still reduce the impact of all these processes by implementing the right health habits even as you age. In addition, finding a routine of play that works for you can help to offset some of the natural aging process.

How are you currently keeping strong?

All humans move from the time they are born (and actually, even before — in utero). Many of these movements were established before we knew what they were — we just began doing them: lifting our heads, sucking our toes, rolling over, sitting up, crawling, walking, running. Most were established from infancy, and we still do them all to the best of our ability — though grabbing our toes gets harder as we get older!

Even if you are limited by injury or illness, your body still wants to move. (See, for example, my interview with Cindy Gorlewski on page 72.)

Strength is an important component of staying flexible and mobile as we age. Everyone loses muscle mass as they get older unless they do some resistance training. In fact, after the age of 30, unless you are in the habit of regularly strengthening your muscles, muscle mass and function starts to decline. Physically inactive people can lose as much as 3 to 5% of their muscle mass each decade after 30. The science shows that whether you use weights in a gym or your own body weight, strength training leads to lifelong functionality, power, and neural coordination.

In a June 2017 article in *Time* magazine, Brad Schoenfeld, assistant professor of exercise science at Lehman College in New York City, stated:

> When you're young, bone resorption is balanced and in some cases exceeded by new bone tissue generation. But later in life, bone tissue losses accelerate and outpace the creation of new

> bone. That acceleration is especially pronounced among people who are sedentary and women who have reached or passed menopause. This loss of bone tissue leads to the weakness and postural problems that plague many older adults.

Simply put, strong muscles mean strong bones, since they are attached to each other. This can reduce the chance of injury and atrophy (muscle depletion) over time. Strong muscles have the added benefit of keeping your metabolism fired up, which helps defend against fat gain, improves insulin sensitivity, and reduces fracture risks as you age.

The adage "use it or lose it" is real — but it doesn't mean it can't be *fun*!

What is the BAM for function?

So what is the bare-ass minimum for functional play? The World Health Organization (WHO) recommends that "muscle-strengthening activities should be done involving major muscle groups on 2 or more days a week." What kind of activities? There is a spectrum, of course, from lifting heavy weights to gardening — anything that requires you carry a heavy load, to trigger enough stress, to challenge your muscles. Unlike cardio, where heart-pumping activity is recommended for at least 20 minutes 5 to 7 days a week (see Chapter 3, starting on page 31),

> **With functional training, no single muscle screams; instead the entire body sings.**
> — JC Santana

no time is specified for muscle-strengthening activities. That's because each of us has a specific "one-rep maximum" (the maximum amount of weight that a person can possibly lift for one repetition).

To determine your maximum, try a push-up. Can you do 1, in good form, or 20? That's your maximum and where you start to build your strength. As you get stronger, you can gradually increase the number of repetitions (8 to 15) and sets you do. A total body strength circuit can take as little as 5 minutes depending on your starting level.

The fitness industry has fancy terms for movements that mimic the way we move in everyday life: *functional training* or *integral strength*. Using the same movements needed to function on a daily basis, you can use your own body weight to build strength and mobility during your playtime.

Nothing fancy, no machines — your body is your machine!

As we saw in Chapter 2, finding an activity you can enjoy and sustain is key. The cool part is that by manipulating the speed or angle at which you move, you can progressively strengthen your muscles. Sure, if and when you want to, you can buy some fun toys to add extra resistance, but it's not a necessity.

DO YOU KNOW ABOUT NEAT?

NEAT stands for "non-exercise activity thermogenesis" — in simple terms, it's the energy we expend doing everything that is *not* sleeping, eating, or formal exercise or sports (so things like cooking, shopping, gardening, standing around, and fidgeting).

Your total energy each day comes from a combination of three things:

1. The rate at which you process/digest the foods you eat (the thermic effect of food): 10%
2. The energy your body requires to function when it's not in motion (your resting or basal metabolic rate [BMR]): 60%
3. Non-exercise activity thermogenesis (NEAT): 30%

Many people mistakenly think that simply doing their regular workout is enough to make a positive change in their overall health. Believe it or not, even if you've managed to get your heart-pumping cardio/FUNctional session in, sitting around all day afterward pretty much cancels out all the benefits you've gained by working out.

The good news is that there is true magic in movement, and it's twofold:

1. You can fire up your resting or basal metabolic rate (BMR) to help you burn energy more efficiently by engaging in resistance training/functional movements and higher-intensity play.
2. You can have a positive impact on your overall health through the type of NEAT things you do during the day.

Have you ever wondered why someone who seems to be following the same exercise regime as you appears to be enjoying better results? Don't blame it on genetics: it's likely due to a marked difference in their NEAT activities. Perhaps the person you are comparing yourself to has simply has a more active job and gets up from their desks more.

So pay attention to your NEAT activities and consider making some changes — stand more often, park your car further away, take the stairs, walk rather than drive. The coolest thing about NEAT is that a subtle but consistent difference in daily activity and lifestyle can add up to a healthier future over time.

Let the world be your gym

Everything you need to move more is right outside your door: stairs, rocks, benches, trees, fences, sidewalks, parking lots, green spaces, concrete jungles … they are *all* functional movement spaces. If exercise is a keystone habit for a healthier life, I want to show you how it can truly be an adventure for your lifetime! Have fun *and* feel good — how great is that?

Functional movement is critical to everyday life. Our bodies don't move in a single direction — we move side to side, backward, forward, and diagonally. You'll want to include all of these movement patterns as you plan and get excited about playing. In the simplest form, the four pillars of functional movement are:

- Push *(upper body)*
- Pull *(upper body)*
- Level change/motion *(lower body)*
- Rotation *(core)*

So how do the four pillars figure into some of our everyday movements? As you can see in the wide-ranging examples on the next page, they often work in tandem.

- Running to catch the bus — Motion.
- Getting in and out of a chair, on and off a toilet, in or out of bed — Level change.
- Going up and down stairs — Level change/motion.
- Walking to the mailbox — Motion.
- Lifting something into the trunk of a car — Level change, rotation, and pull/push.
- Operating a wheelchair — Push/pull/motion.
- Opening a door — Push or pull.
- Moving a couch from one side of a room to another — Push/pull/motion/rotation.
- Arranging rocks in the garden — Level change, push, pull, and rotation.
- Helping a friend out of a pool — Pull/level change.
- Monkey-bars at the playground with your kid — Pull/push.
- Putting on a seat belt in the car — Rotation.
- Getting the lid off a jar — Push/rotation.
- Spinning while you dance — Rotation (and if you dip: level change).
- Throwing a ball, golfing, playing baseball, swinging your kid around in circles — Push, pull, level change, and rotation!

To continue enjoying, and being able to do, your daily activities as you age — things like getting out of bed, lifting your groceries, or reaching for something on the floor — try seeing them as forms of functional movement.

Remember, the point is that it's not just formal exercise that counts — **all movement matters!** The minute you start to understand that your body doesn't know whether you are at a fitness centre in workout clothes or bundled up outside shovelling snow, the more free you will feel. Once we become aware of the muscles we are engaging, those movements become purposeful. Even 30 minutes a day of light activity like household chores and walking for errands lowers the risk of dying early by 12%.

> **We don't stop playing because we grow old, we grow old because we stop playing.**
> —George Bernard Shaw

You don't need to go out of your way to practice functional movements. For example, think about the way you use your legs to push yourself off the bed when you get up in the morning. Instead of just getting off the bed and leaving, sit back down and push yourself off again. There, you've done a squat. It really can be that simple. (See page 76 on the beginner's mindset for more details on this method.)

WHAT THE EXPERTS SAY

Cindy Gorlewski

Cindy Gorlewski's true love is teaching. She has a BA/BPHE from Queen's University and a Bachelor of Education from the University of Toronto. A secondary school physical education specialist, Cindy went on to get an MBA at Western. She taught core French in the York Catholic District School Board and coached track and boys basketball. In 1988, Cindy started experiencing the first symptoms of multiple sclerosis (MS). Despite her challenges, she has continued to practice functional movement by adapting play into her life. Cindy now uses a manual wheelchair full time and hangs out at physiotherapy a lot. Cindy continued to teach and raise three children, but it became a physical struggle and she opted for long-term disability in 2000.

JO: Have you felt self-conscious because of your MS?

CG: Yeah. But you have to get past the thing where your pride goes, "Ooh, I can't be like that in front of people." I did that — I hid away after I went on disability. I didn't go to the mall for two years. I was a teacher, it's a small community, and you're always seeing people you know. I'd go out of town and nobody would know me there. But then I went, "Aw, this is stupid."

I didn't go to a family reunion for years until my Aunt Liz said, "We all know. I don't know what you're trying to hide. If you think by not coming you're not the centre of conversation you're completely wrong."

I said the same thing to a guy whose got Parkinson's. He was a football player at Queen's University and in my phys. ed. class. When we had our last reunion, I said "You know, we all know. So you'll be the centre of conversation whether you're sitting there or not. You're better to come and just let us see you. We don't care. We want to see YOU!"

You have to get to a place of self-acceptance.

JO: And does shared experience help with that?

CG: Yeah. I have support and really good friends. We all have MS and met in a chat room years ago. We see each other for lunch. One of them, I talk to every day. They get it. Even the dark humour! Like if you go, "Oh, my bladder's acting up today," everyone knows what that means.

JO: Has your level and kind of physical activity changed over the years?

CG: I don't swim anymore because it's too cold and makes me go very rigid. And to be honest, it's too much trouble — especially changing. When I'm dressed, I'm dressed for the day because it's a big hassle.

I love weights. I used to walk into the gym with a cane or two canes and do weight training once a week on Friday night. It was empty, there was nobody looking at me, and I could get on every machine. But there came a point when I had to give that up.

And, of course, operating my wheelchair is a workout.

JO: What is in your plan for practicing functionality?

CG: I have a standing frame. I go to physio once a week at a place that deals almost exclusively with neurological stuff. There are a lot of people in wheelchairs and with canes; there are a lot who've had strokes, brain injury, or accidents; there are lots with MS — whatever you can think of, it's there. We practice some functionality there, and I try to bring that home. Simple things like rolling over in bed, moving from a sitting position to the standing frame, and other things that are part of my day-to-day routine.

JO: What benefits do you get from using your standing frame?

CG: I need this to stand. I need this for my circulation. I need this for my organs to be back to where they should be. That's functional. You sit in a wheelchair long enough your organs come out the front. Your diaphragm doesn't work. When I'm standing it just opens things up. It works on the bowels. It works on the bladder. It works on your lungs. It works on your heart. It works on your blood vessels. There are so many advantages to standing. *Just* standing. Nothing else.

Not everyone who is disabled can use a standing frame — luckily I have tone in my legs and I can. There are standing frames where you can practice going from a little bit of a bend to a full stand, but this one is easier for me to get in and out of, which was more important since it meant I would use it more often.

My goal is to stand for an hour a day. It's a very tough thing to do.

JO: What would you see as a potential "barrier" to accomplishing that?

CG: My whole life is appointments — osteopath, chiropractor, physio every week, possibly another physio that deals with spinal cord injuries and functionality … It makes it very difficult because everything is timed in my life. When I drink my coffee is timed, when I go to the bathroom is timed. Everything is timed and often can't be changed. So scheduling in an hour of standing time can be a challenge.

JO: What functional movement is a highlight for you?

CG: It's not about big motion or movement or anything like that. I still get the *Globe and Mail* on Saturdays because I love the crossword puzzle. Roman, my husband, says, "but you could do that online," and I say, "Yes, I could, and I could press a button and type in the letters, but I want the pen in my hand to make the fine motor movement for as long as possible." Even if it might not be the neatest writing in the world. If I give it up, I won't be able to do it.

DON'T RESIST!

Many people are put off by the idea of weight or resistance training because they think it's too hard. Women in particular are also concerned about bulking up, but they shouldn't be concerned: Women aren't built to gain serious mass because we don't have the same testosterone level in our muscles as men do. What women I've worked with *do* gain is self-confidence because it feels good to be able to lift heavy things — like three bags of groceries rather than one.

Technique matters a lot with functional training, so I do recommend that you consider consulting a qualified professional who can help you with form and technique as you expand your interest in play and add equipment to your regimen. Furthermore, a professional can set out the guidelines for reaching your objectives and help identify what your limits are.

Embrace a beginner's mindset

Approaching functional movements as if you've never tried them before opens you to learning something new about a familiar action and to experiencing the remarkable way your body responds. When we embrace that idea — without judgment and without taking ourselves too seriously — magic happens. In fact, it might just change your attitude about strength exercise and inject a sense of fun even when you're doing basic activities (like taking the stairs instead of the elevator and then working up to being able to do walking lunges as you go).

Do you ever really think about sitting in a chair or pay attention to what muscles you are using? Probably not. You most likely just do it without much thought or analysis. Well, let's use this as an example and break it down as the functional movement that it is.

Here's how to sit in a chair with a beginner's mindset.

1. Start by standing in front of the seat of a chair. Place your feet shoulder-width apart. Feel the muscles of your feet, your calves, your legs and butt. Feel the alignment of your spine, your shoulders over your hips and your ears over your shoulders. Look straight ahead. Excellent posture check built in right there — tricky, huh?

2. Squeeze the muscles in your legs and butt for a second. Okay, there they are.

3. Now, slowly and with control (let's take 5 seconds here to go slowly), move your butt back down toward the seat while paying attention to your body weight being more in the heels of your feet than in

the toes. When you do this, your weight will shift back rather than forward into your knees. (If your weight is too far forward, you'll feel as if you are falling forward and you'll strain the muscles in your legs and feel some discomfort in your knees.)

4. As your butt moves back, you bend at the waist and your chest tilts slightly toward the floor.
5. When you are almost in the chair, you might feel a slight burn in your legs — those are your muscles saying "Hi!"
6. Set your butt toward the front of the chair seat. We are going to stay at the front of the chair to stand up.

Let's do the opposite and stand up:

1. Starting toward the front of the chair, keep those feet shoulder-width apart and toes straight (if they flare slightly in or out, that's okay — it has to do with the muscle alignment in your hips). Make sure you are sitting up tall — ears in line with shoulders, shoulders in line with hips. Your hips and knees are parallel to the floor.
2. Plant your feet firmly on the floor.
3. Push up through the heels of your feet.

4. Now, slowly and with control — let's take 5 seconds here to go slowly — feel your leg and butt muscles start to engage as you slowly stand up. And with that, you've just completed a "squat" movement pattern. Look at you go!

(Head on over to **janetomstead.com** for a visual of this move.)

Start with small increments

If you already have a play routine, but it doesn't include strength exercises, could you commit to adding some functional movement? It can be anything you can successfully repeat without injury — for example, chair squats like I just mentioned or balancing on one foot while you brush your teeth. If you attach the functional movement to a routine or behaviour you already do, it's easy to incorporate more play into your day.

For incremental increase, look for other opportunities to practice the habit. Let's take standing up from your desk, for example:

- When your phone rings, stand up. While speaking, keep standing and do some calf raises — great for balance.
- When someone comes into your office, stand up (then sit back down or keep standing).

I have a client who uses washroom breaks during the day as an opportunity to practice functional movement. Every time she returns to her desk, she does 10 squats. If she takes 5 washroom breaks and does 10 squats every time, she will have performed 50 squats by the end of the day!

If you're finding it hard to think of when to add functional activities, go back to your "time-out line" and review your daily activities (see page 156). Can you identify an activity that would allow you to fit in some strength training? Once you get your mind — and body — working this way, you'll soon see how to increase these mini exercise moments and playtimes. Add these elements in small increments over a period of time.

USE IT!

If we were meant to live our lives on couches and in chairs, our bodies would be shaped like throw pillows. Those feet (and legs!) of yours were made for walkin'— not to mention dancing, cycling, and hiking. And those arms were made for activities like lifting, digging, throwing, and pulling your body through the water (aka swimming). Pick an activity you really enjoy and do it.

Variety is key

When it comes to a strategy that will give you the biggest bang for your buck, variety is essential. In real life we rarely use just one muscle — in most cases, our muscles have to work together to produce the movements that we regard as easy, like picking up a child, reaching for the laundry in the dryer, or putting away the groceries.

One successful approach I've used with clients to introduce variety is assigning to each day a different play move that focuses on a different functional body part. The idea is to do as many repetitions as you can with good form to "failure." *Failure* means that you can't possibly do one more — your muscles are "feeling the burn." For some people that could be one; for others it might be three sets of 12 to 15 repetitions. Remember the 10% rule in the last chapter? The same applies here, too: Try 5 push-ups 2 times per week and continue at that level for a couple of weeks until 5 becomes easy, then add another one (10%). If you start with 5, and add 1 more every other week for a year, you'd be able to do over 100 push-ups in 365 days. *Holy moly* that's cool, simple, and functional!

Check out the table on the next page for an example of how to incorporate functional play into your days.

Use music to motivate you

Day	Functional move	Body focus	Functional pillar
Monday	Countertops (push-ups)	Chest	Push
Wednesday	Supermans (back)	Back	Pull
Friday	Step ups (lunges)	Legs	Level change/ Motion
Saturday	Standing up (knee lifts)	Core	Rotation

For visual examples, head over to **youtube.com/@janetomstead**.

Mobility matters

Mobility is a sign of how well our bodies are able to move and recover. In order for us to keep mobile, we need to practice recovery movements that incorporate flexibility "stretching." Some people might have muscle imbalances, which can cause them to be inflexible and less mobile. Stretching helps to increase the range of motion in your joints during activities while reducing pain and tightness in your muscles.

The World Health Organization says: "In older adults with poor mobility, there is consistent evidence that regular physical activity is safe and reduces risk of falls by nearly 30%. For prevention of falls, most evidence supports a physical activity pattern of balance training and moderate-intensity muscle-strengthening activities three times per week."

TO STRETCH OR NOT TO STRETCH

One of the greatest debates in the fitness world is "to stretch or not to stretch?" The answer is: it's a personal preference. Some people like to stretch before they exercise; others like to stretch afterward. And there are various types of stretching you can do, too:

Static stretching — when you hold a stretch in a challenging but comfortable position for between 10 to 30 seconds — is the most common form of stretching and is used for improving overall flexibility.

Dynamic stretching — when you complete a series of motions repeatedly — loosens up joints and muscles.

Foam rolling — when you self-massage — helps to release tension in the soft tissues around the muscles (called fascia).

Functional movements are great for strengthening your muscles and increasing your mobility. But you also have to pump your heart with regular cardiovascular exercise (see page 160). And that's an easy one to introduce into your daily activities — take a brisk walk or use stairs whenever it's practical and possible.

CHOOSE YOUR 5-MINUTE FUNCTION

Complete the assessment on page 160 to figure out how to introduce 5-minute functional movement playtimes into your day — either before your heart-pumping cardio or after.

What happens when you stop playing

My dad was an amazing role model for the entire family. He enjoyed playing and took part in all sorts of sports such as golf, skiing, tennis, and squash. I think he liked these sports mostly because they engaged him in physical movement and relationship building. My dad had a huge circle of friends. The one thing he didn't do was "practice" for these sports in the off-season. Had he been in the practice of using functional movement patterns to help him keep strong and agile for these sports, I don't think he would have tossed in the towel so early.

I noticed that in his mid-70s, my dad slowly gave up playing his favourite sports, and I think it came down to ego and lack of self-confidence. You see, once he started losing the muscle strength and agility he once had naturally at a younger age, he couldn't play like he used to. So he stopped. His ego got in the way. And because he stopped and also had not cultivated the habit of keeping his muscles strong, he got weaker. Once Dad got weaker, his world got so much smaller. His death at 83 resulted from the slow and steady decline of a once healthy and active man. Learn from my dad: practice playing!

SURPRISINGLY USEFUL: FIDGETING

Fidgeting is a functional movement. Yup, that innocuous, low-intensity activity we're often unaware of — jiggling a leg, tapping a foot, fiddling with a lock of hair — burns energy and keeps blood flowing to our extremities. If you notice you're doing any of these things, don't be too quick to bounce them from your repertoire of movements. Fidgeting is part of your NEAT — non-exercise activity thermogenesis.

Do what you love

My 25-year-old client Sam is a perfect example of someone who doesn't like going to the gym. Despite feeling like a fish out of water, she kept paying the monthly fee because she knew she *should* be working out. When we discussed this in a coaching meeting, she said the things she loved to do the most were walking and dancing — both excellent for staving off disease by keeping her heart strong. After our conversation, she gave up her gym membership. A couple of months later, when she was ready, she started to add 5 minutes of functional movement at the end of her walk ... or the beginning ... or in the middle — timing didn't matter. What mattered was that she consistently challenged her muscles a couple of times a week. She has seamlessly added this to her routine. In fact, she now adds functional movement to her life every other day. And since she's on the go, so is her workout: Sam does the moves I listed on page 82 (lunges up the stairs, squats, push-ups, supermans, and standing knee touches) during commercial breaks when she's watching television. Bingo! Habit established.

You can do this, too!

Once you realize your mindset has shifted from *having to* do something functional to *getting to* do it, you are beginning to adopt a play-based mindset and are on your way to a healthier you. What does that feel like? People who are in a better physical state see play — movement and function — beyond the walls of a gym. Movement is part of everyday life. You'll see that incorporating small movements into your day everyday, until it becomes a habit will help you enjoy life more mindfully and fully. Making sure that the type of play you choose aligns with your values (see "The Value of Play," starting on page 13) will help you keep on track as well as determine your motivation (see pages 164–167).

WHAT THE EXPERTS SAY

Juan Carlos Santana

Juan Carlos "JC" Santana is the Founder and Director of the Institute of Human Performance (**ihpfit.com**), a state-of-the-art training facility in Boca Raton, Florida. JC is a dynamic speaker (over 300 major conferences in the fitness industry and counting), a sought-after consultant, and the prolific author of over 70 DVDs and 17 books in the area of fitness and performance enhancement. His latest two books with Human Kinetics, *Functional Training* and *JC's Total Body Transformation* have been translated into 8 different languages and are being used as textbooks by dozens of universities across the globe.

JC has been referred to as the "leading practitioner of functional fitness." A graduate of Florida Atlantic University with bachelors and master's degrees in exercise science, JC is currently working on his Ph.D. in exercise physiology. He has served on the National Strength and Conditioning Association (NSCA) board of directors, and as the editor of the sport-specific training column for the *NSCA Journal*. As a college professor, he has taught sports training systems, strength training, and strength and conditioning for the combat athlete at Florida Atlantic University (FAU). He is currently involved in ongoing research projects with several international universities.

JO: In simplifying the science of movement, which exercises/movements do you consider most important for healthy living?

JC: The most important functional movements are the four pillars of human movement: locomotion, level changes, push–pull, and rotations. The most basic exercises that evaluate and train the pillars are the eight exercises I use to evaluate and improve the four pillars: one-legged anterior reach, one-legged squat, two-legged parallel stance squat, alternating lunge, push-up, recline pull, rotations with pivots, rotations without pivots. (For a visual demonstration, go to **youtube.com/@janetomstead**.)

JO: Do you adapt movements for different people?

JC: Look at both an athlete lowering the level and a mother working around the house picking up things. When you look at their back position, it's often very similar! What does that tell you? One person might be moving fast or picking up something heavy, another may move slowly and pick up something light. However, since all of us deal with the same structures of the body, we all use the same movements (i.e., the four pillars).

Let's use the reaching lunge as an example: For a tennis player, that move is equal to a low volley. For an elderly person, it's like tying shoelaces. Everybody should be able to do a reaching lunge. It's just the speed (which is the momentum) and the range of motion and load that's different to meet the demand for that person's lifestyle and their capabilities. First you have to determine ability and then match it with proper movement (difficulty of skill and intensity of load).

JO: What's a simple way to understand the four pillars of movement?

JC: You're doing the pillars every day — that's what the body does naturally — *it's function*. It's like your car's function: the car moves forward, back, right, and left, all being directed by the steering wheel. All cars move and function the same way, regardless of horsepower and body design. All bodies are the same way — all move around using the four pillars. You tie your shoelace: bingo, level change and reach (push)! You throw a football: you're doing all four pillars. Walking around an obstacle on the sidewalk: you are using *all four pillars!* And if you look at locomotion, it's got all four pillars: As you take your stride, you change your level slightly, one arm goes forward, the opposite leg goes forward — so there is your push and pull (that counterbalances the lower body) — and when that happens, you rotate your torso.

I use the pillars to describe how the body moves. And I recommend doing exercises from each of the pillars so we can move our bodies the way they are intended to move.

JO: What would be your first piece of advice to somebody who is extremely inactive but who wants to start a more active lifestyle?

JC: Start small! Everybody thinks you have to start walking for 15, 20, 30 minutes. You don't have to. Start with 5 minutes. Can you walk for 5 minutes? Yeah, but why bother? Because you start establishing a behaviour. Take your time! Everybody wants to walk 30 minutes right off the bat and of course they get hurt so they don't walk. Can you walk for 5 minutes, 7 days this week? Walk around the kitchen for 5 minutes and then sit down, done. Your homework is done. And then next week, add 2 minutes, and then repeat every week after that. In 3 months, look where you're going to be and you won't even feel it.

JO: What if you're in a wheelchair?

JC: Still look at the pillars. If you have the ability, work the upper body. Wheel the chair forward, wheel it backward ... forward and backward! Get yourself a band, attach it to something. Pull on it, push on it, rotate it from every angle you can imagine. Can you get into a pool? Then get a buoyancy belt and swim your ass off, letting your feet hang if they don't work. If you can get on the floor, do some modified supermans or something like that, or get on the floor prone, side and supine and move your limbs. It's finding ways to work out with what you've got.

JO: How do you see physical activity connected to our overall well-being?

JC: For me, exercise is physical prayer. I've seen the connection between physical effort and the spiritual transformation that people undergo. The body is a physical manifestation of our emotions, and as we start exercising, we have to evaluate the feeling. Exercise is the trigger by which you feel the effort. Each new level of effort is a new emotion. It's like a new taste in food — we know food but maybe we don't know broccoli. Something different!

Everybody will discover something when they exercise. The first thing might be a "feeling" of discomfort. And then, *Wait ... okay! What is that? Oh, it hurts. I'm tired!* I say, "Okay, let's talk about that." You tell me you have a past history that maybe you developed when you were totally out of shape and you tried to run track — that when you feel like this, you throw up and you don't want to do that anymore. And I'll say, "Well, 1) this ain't track, 2) you ain't 12, and 3) you're not taking off for the 400! This is an experience." It's a sensation you defined according to your old story. This old story does not serve the new you anymore — let it go and see this for what is: something new! *Don't judge it!*

The whole idea is to take the moment and say to yourself, *What is this? Oh, it's accelerated metabolism, it's accelerated energy.* Great! Why? *Because I'm in a state where I'm doing accelerated energy and it's my new normal.*

JO: How do we stay in the moment?

JC: The first thing we teach is relax the face! It's symbolic for staying in the present moment and "not judging a feeling according to some outdated belief." Just feel what you feel and that's it. Period. You can't give up an opportunity because you projected into the future — because you thought to yourself, *I'm gonna get tired.*

Say the trigger — the goal — is the 8th rep. As we're getting close to that, I tell them it's coming so I need them to stay with me. They'll go like this [scrunched face] 'cause they want it. And then I'll say, "Relax the face." All of a sudden, they go really relaxed and you see them go into a safe place. *Bam, bam, bam,* they do 12 reps like nothing.

It's a way to be able to experience every rep, every minute of each activity. How can you practice something 700, 800, 900 times mindfully per week and not change as an individual? It's impossible.

A year from now you may wish you had started today.

—Karen Lamb

MOVEMENT
IGNITES
NEUROLOGICAL
DEPTH

Your brain on play

What if your doctor pulled out a prescription pad and wrote "Daily Exercise"? Would you take a written prescription more seriously than simply being told you have to exercise once a day? And what if your doctor told you that not following the prescription could lead to an earlier death?

Most of us would take it pretty seriously. But for many people, even when they've accepted that bleak reality, the choice to move a little more is tough. Often it's because they don't know where to start or they have a physical limitation that prevents them from getting active.

Perhaps we've become immune to the studies that show we are more sedentary and that this is having a negative effect on our lives. But if we become ill and the doctor prescribes medication, most of us are happy to follow the doctor's orders. If we think of movement as medicine that will help us be healthier, we might find it easier to set aside that initial 1 minute a day and eventually turn it into 20 minutes or more.

Play is nature's therapy — so how do we get started?

It starts with your brain

The brain is one of the most mysterious parts of our body. It's not like a muscle or bone, but it's connected to what happens throughout the body — like a central control station or a hard drive on a computer. Neuroscientist Wendy Suzuki gives an inspiring TED Talk called "The Brain-Changing Effects of Exercise" about the transformative powers of our brains. She enthusiastically breaks down the scientific details on how exercise helps your brain grow and how, over the long term, it can "protect your brain from incurable diseases." I encourage you to watch it — it's only 2 minutes and 15 seconds long.

It's been shown that different functional and cardiovascular movements affect different parts of the brain — like medicine for the brain. When you're moving more, your blood starts pumping, triggering growth in the hippocampus, the core area where emotions, learning, and memory storage take place.

Every improvement in any part of your personality or performance boosts your self-esteem and causes you to like and respect yourself even more.
—Meiko S. Patton

Move to protect your brain

PLAY TO IMPROVE YOUR MOOD

Focusing on the mental benefits of moving your body can actually make you more likely to do it again. Sergio Pellis, a professor in the Department of Neuroscience at the University of Lethbridge, Alberta, studies how play shapes behaviour and mood in the newer part of the mind (evolutionarily speaking), the prefrontal cortex, which controls behaviour and the ability to solve problems. "One of the things about play is, it's hard to do it and not be in a better mood," says Pellis. "Playing fosters the kinds of neurochemical changes in your brain and body that tend to counteract the effect of neurochemicals produced when you're stressed or unhappy."

Next time you are finished your playtime, take note of your mood and feeling of awesomeness!

If you want to get the blood flowing more quickly, the easiest way is to increase the intensity at which you walk each day or week. Remember those "time-out" increments (see page 156)! Heart-pumping cardio helps protect your brain from the effects of aging. A 2018 study published in the *Journal of Neurology* reveals that "women who were physically fit in middle age were roughly 88% less likely to develop dementia (defined as a decline in memory severe enough to interfere with daily life) than their peers who were only moderately fit."

Another good activity that gets more blood to your brain is functional movement. As mentioned in the previous chapter, you don't have to go to a gym to do this. You can do simple exercises at home using, for example, cans of tomatoes, or splurge on some small weights that you can tuck away by the television and grab while watching your favourite shows. Done in a circuit style, these moves raise your heart rate.

THE POWER OF WALKING

Children and adults alike can gain mood-boosting benefits, brain function, and cognition in a simple 20-minute walk. Just getting up off the couch or away from your desk is key. You can do it!

Other options for supporting brain activity include sports drills, yoga, and aerobic exercise. Depending on your circumstances, these can be done at home, but you might want to take a few classes to get you started (and let's not underestimate the power of the social connections you'll make if you do). When we practice exercise we like, the brain turns on its magic brain-derived neurotropic factor (BDNF), which helps fresh neurons to develop and shape new networks. That means moving a little more certainly can improve your mind and sharpen your memory.

Sports drills affect specific parts of the brain: the basal ganglia (for movement), parietal lobe (sensory perception and information), and cerebellum (such as balance, posture, speech, and motor control). Yoga, known as the discipline for thoughts and emotions, affects the frontal lobe and, deep in the brain, the insula and amygdala to calm anxiety and fear. The part of the brain that is the core for memory and learning, the hippocampus, responds best to aerobic exercise. So heart-pumping play directly influences your memory. Keeping variety in your play routine is of benefit to your whole brain.

THE EFFECTS OF PLAY-BASED MOVEMENT ON CHILDREN

I have seen the brain-altering effects on mood and memory happen right before my eyes in the work I've done over the years at LifeSports. Back in 2004 when LifeSports was born, both my business partner, Kym Grippo, and I saw a need to help educators introduce fun, innovative ways to get kids active.

Our objective was twofold: 1) to introduce kids and teachers (from grades 4 through 12) to a way of exercise that felt like play, and in doing so 2) to fire up their neurotransmitters and movement patterns, which would increase their ability to focus in class. After playing with and coaching thousands of students, we had a ton of amazing feedback from teachers telling us how the kids were more focused in class than ever. It really does work!

In fact, research has repeatedly shown that children need opportunities to move. As Lara N. Dotson-Renta stated in her article for *The Atlantic*, "Memory and movement are linked, and the body is a tool of learning, not a roadblock to or a detour away from it."

Laying the mind/muscle groundwork in childhood sets the stage for greater play ability in adulthood. When someone — no matter the age — realizes that play can be rewarding, enriching, and purposeful, exercise can become an important part of the way they live.

Get and stay motivated

So you're not an athlete, that's okay. It turns out that your mindset (or internal dialogue) is as important to success as your physical fitness. If you believe you can, you will. Finding something that motivates you and feeds a positive mindset is key.

There are two types of motivation: intrinsic (self-motivation) and extrinsic (external motivation). When you find an activity that you love and it immediately has an internal positive effect, making you want to keep doing it and even do it more, that's intrinsic motivation. For example, a client of mine is intrinsically motivated to follow her program because: 1) she likes to have a plan, and 2) she finds the process personally satisfying and it gives her a sense of pride. Her values are aligned with being active and she looks forward to the activity because it's joyful. Those who are intrinsically motivated tend to continue exercising because it's enjoyable.

But what if we don't like "exercise" even when it's play-based? Sometimes we are more driven by outside rewards. For example, one of my clients likes to sign up for 10-kilometre races because he likes the thought of receiving a medal at the end.

Find and use what works for you! Extrinsic motivators may get us going when we lack intrinsic motivation.

A little self-compassion goes a long way

We all talk to ourselves in our heads. Is your internal dialogue positive, supporting your activity efforts, or negative, focusing on your mistakes? Is your brain working for or against you? Self-esteem is an essential emotional component if we are to achieve our potential in life.

> **The brain responds like muscles do, growing with use, withering with inactivity.**
> —John J. Ratey

Sometimes getting real about our current play situation sucks — it's not fun facing the self-loathing and shame that comes with putting off something that's difficult. Sure, you can procrastinate or go into denial, pretending it won't catch up with you, but eventually, not moving a little more *will* catch up with you. You'll find yourself in a state of far more diminished physical and mental well-being that might have been prevented. If feelings of failure and shame are part of the baggage you bring with your good intentions to do a little more, do a little better, and change your play habit, unpack and air them out!

For example, negative self-talk such as "Oh sure, I can try but everyone will laugh at me" or "I'm so out of shape why even bother" can certainly stand in your way. Be compassionate with yourself — the way you would be with a child making the effort you're about to — and turn that talk on its head: "Okay, if I try and everyone laughs at me, I'll just keep going and they'll have nothing to laugh at" or "Okay, I'm out of shape, but if I start by doing something really simple, I can become a winner who can then build a habit I'll be proud of!"

Start small

Yes, I've said this before, but I'm saying it again: start with small steps! Overdoing it with too much too soon will only earn you aches, pains, and even injuries. Instead, picture improving your life based on the idea of "a little more, a little better." What does that look like?

Perhaps you like to walk yet find it hard to consistently walk for a certain length of time. What does a little more walking look like? My 87-year-old client (who still goes to the office) has decided that walking after lunch at work is a habit that he can sustain. Adding his activity (walking) to another habit (lunch time) makes his task effortless. When he finishes his lunch, he puts on his running shoes and takes a 20-minute walk, indoors or outdoors (depending on the weather). Another client of mine takes public transit to work and back every day. She's decided that on the transit (bus, subway) she stands and when there is a choice to take an escalator or stairs, she takes the stairs. Adding small changes to a routine she's already doing is automatically adding more play into her day, effortlessly.

If you take the escalator most of the time when you're commuting, can you take the stairs a little more often? Perhaps one extra time a week? Then the next week, two extra times? The week after that, three extra times? Build from there ... a little more, a little better.

You want to make sure you're able to handle the slow and steady progress you'll make. As keen as you are to go hard once you've made up your mind to start, please resist the temptation. Your body needs to adapt to its new workload. I can't emphasize enough to start slowly. Only you can set the pace — just be ultra-conservative in the beginning if it's been a while.

Don't limit yourself

Your brain might be playing mind games with you. This isn't the kind of play we want when those games reinforce negative thoughts and feelings. Examine the story you're telling yourself about your health. What can you control or not control about your current situation? What is the cost of not changing? Denial definitely carries a cost.

Sometimes the things we fear doing are most often the things we need to do. Maybe it's time to stop the negative internal dialogue. What about finding your superpowers? We all have superpowers (we'll discuss this more on page 162). Instead of limiting yourself to the "to do's" of the day, how about reframing that list into the "ta da's!"? (Check out my interview with Lisanne in the next chapter for more on this idea.)

UNDERSTAND YOUR LIMITING BELIEFS AND SUPERPOWERS

It's important to understand both your limiting beliefs and your superpowers. Complete the chart on page 162 to help you figure out what is preventing you from taking that important first step toward more play.

Every effort equals progress

I can't stress enough the importance of continuing to have a beginner's mindset while you approach your new play habits. Progress happens just by starting and then consistently showing up. Every day your energy level and mood will be different — because that's life. Look at your efforts as progress.

As you continue progressing, you can add more variety, time, or intensity, but only when you've established a consistent habit. Keeping a written or photo journal of your progress helps to cement the fact that you are still showing up. There are varied schools of thought about how long it takes for a new habit to stick, but a generally accepted time frame for behaviours to become habits is 5 to 12 weeks.

The mind–body connection

In his bestselling book *Spark: The Revolutionary New Science of Exercise and the Brain*, Harvard Medical School psychiatry professor Dr. John Ratey not only preaches the benefits of moderate- to high-intensity cardiovascular exercise but also scientifically proves them in a number of high schools throughout the United States. The benefits are physical as well as psychological, the idea being that physical exercise turns our brains on and the side effects help our bodies to be healthy.

You yourself, as much as anybody in the entire universe, deserve your love and affection.
—Buddha

His book finds further support for the mind–body connection since exercise can help you be more social, reduce anxiety, fight depression, utilize your body's ability to burn energy more efficiently, improve focus for conditions like ADHD, combat addictions, help you make better healthy-life decisions (regarding impulsive actions such as smoking, overeating, and overspending), and improve a mother's ability to have healthier babies.

Dr. Ratey's work was driven by firsthand accounts of patients who could no longer run after the Boston Marathon bombing. A number of people he saw were experiencing, for the first time, psychological disorders such as depression and ADHD because they couldn't run. Unbeknown to them, running had been their self-medicating method to manage these disorders until they couldn't run anymore. He concluded that exercise was "like taking a little bit of Prozac, and a little bit of Ritalin."

Play reduces anxiety

Depression and anxiety can express itself in many ways: from mild "blues" through to the more seriously debilitating "can't get out of bed." When we feel like this, the last thing we want to do is play or exercise, or even move. However, a 1999 Duke University study on exercise and depression found that "depressed adults who did 45 minutes of aerobic exercise three times a week improved their mood as much as did those who took the prescription anti-depressant Zoloft instead of exercising." The idea is that when you focus on walking instead of your worry, your body naturally releases more of the positive hormones such as serotonin and endorphins, which enhance your mood, while simultaneously reducing production of cortisol, the stress hormone.

My family has had personal experience with the direct relationship between play and anxiety. A few years ago, at the age of 19, my daughter was bedridden from what seemed like a mystery illness. After multiple tests, the doctors concluded it was vertigo. These dizzy spells prohibited

> **We suffer more often in imagination than in reality.**
> —Seneca

her from her favourite form of play — running. In fact, she couldn't even stand for long periods of time. Not being able to move for months contributed to her anxiety, and her anxiety made the dizziness and other physical symptoms even worse. Her mental health deteriorated so much that she ended up in the psychiatric emergency room. Thankfully, my daughter was able to take medication and work with mental health professionals to substantially improve her health and well-being. Years later, my daughter still has an anxiety disorder, but she now also has the tools to manage it. And what's her main tool? Play. She worked her way back to being able to move more every day. Her story proved to me that the mind–body does work together — sometimes for the worse, but more often for the better.

We have control over how we use our body and the ways we can make it more active, in turn improving our brain function. There really is power in positive thinking.

WHAT THE EXPERTS SAY

Dr. John Ratey

John J. Ratey, MD, is an Associate Clinical Professor of Psychiatry at Harvard Medical School, an internationally recognized expert in neuro psychiatry, and a bestselling author.

Dr. Ratey has embarked on a world-wide mission to re-engineer schools, corporations, and individual lifestyle practices by incorporating exercise to achieve peak performance and optimum mental health. A highly sought-after speaker, Dr. Ratey has lectured extensively throughout the world, and his work is frequently profiled in the media.

Dr. Ratey has published over 60 peer-reviewed articles and 11 books translated into 15 languages, including the groundbreaking series "Driven to Distraction" with Dr. Edward Hallowell. With the publication of *Spark: The Revolutionary New Science of Exercise and the Brain*, Dr. Ratey established himself as one of the world's foremost authorities on the brain–fitness connection. His more recent book, *Go Wild*, explores how we can achieve optimal physical and mental health by getting in touch with our caveman roots, and how we can "re-wild" our lives.

JO: What's the best approach to exercise for people with a chronic disease?

JR: It's best for them to go slowly and to first build up their endurance as much as they can. And while they're doing that, to pay attention to strength training and to balance training. Balance especially is so important in the development of an exercise program and getting more fit and less frail. Adding things on as time goes by will get them to the point of being more adventuresome and trying different things once they build up a reservoir of fitness.

JO: What causes the shift from exercise being something we need to do to something we want to do?

JR: Over time, people recognize that they feel so much better when they exercise. They feel more vigorous. They feel more alive. They feel more "with it." They're more attentive. They're more fun. They're more social. Science has proven it, and we see it happening with our kids, with our psychiatric patients of all sorts, and with chronically ill people. Being more social is a major thing. I think people often miss how important it is to be involved with others — we call it vitamin C or "connection." Being connected to one another is healing in itself. It is so important because it keeps us moving forward.

JO: How does play figure into our ongoing development?

JR: All of us are born with a need to play and a drive to play. All mammals play. They play with their brothers and sisters or their parents, but they play. When they don't play their brains are smaller, they're dumber, they don't fit in. If you eliminate play from baby rats and mice, their brains are smaller. They are not very sharp and they don't fit in — they become the bullies or the bullied. We naturally have a need to play and move, and this will drive us to explore different ways of getting our ya-ya's on.

JO: How would you describe the relationship between the body and the brain?

JR: I think that if you get your body in shape, your mind or your brain will follow. Basically, when you use your body, and use it consistently, you're driving your brain not only to follow the movement patterns and get better (for example, at dance or tai chi or taekwondo or tennis or soccer), but also to get better in all those other ways we use our brain (for example, in reading, learning a new language, doing math). By playing games or getting yourself more fit, you increase your ability to learn, to take in, store, remember, use, and search for information — you get smarter.

JO: Does movement help with mental health issues?

JR: I was immediately tuned to how exercise helped my patients or people with various psychiatric problems like depression, anxiety, over response to stress, ADD, autism. All these areas are very much affected by an exercise regimen. We're seeing papers coming out about exercise benefits for autism, schizophrenia, even bipolar disorder.

Hippocrates wrote about the benefit of exercise for depression and for raising the mood. Study after study from almost every country in the world shows that exercise is probably one of the best ways to treat depression as well as avoid getting into the depressive state. I'm working with a non-profit that is using exercise to help addicts reduce cravings and stay sober. We have lots of evidence that this happens with many different addictions. It's a universal treatment that is magical in many ways — and it's fairly free.

JO: Is that news to people?

JR: The big surprise is that people aren't aware of how potent exercise is. Exercise-as-medicine movements started in the U.S. and are now happening around the world.

If you're undergoing cancer treatment, aside from the medical interventions, the number-one treatment recommendation is to get exercise. It helps protect against mood changes, keys up your immune system, and bolsters your feeling of motivation to continue with your life.

I think the biggest impact that exercise has shown is with Parkinson's disease. It is now the number-one recommendation for somebody diagnosed with the disease. A group called Delay the Disease offers a program to stop the progression of Parkinson's by getting exercise and staying exercised, with personal trainers and boot camps for Parkinson's patients.

JO: Which exercise or movement do you consider essential for optimal living?

JR: There isn't really one that I would say is primary or the only thing to do. Endurance, strength training, and balance: they all interface with one another, and I think you have to do all of them. As you age, your muscles go away, so strength training is important. Also, with age, your balance goes away but you can train that up better than any other problem that you might have.

JO: What can help keep us motivated to exercise?

JR: The way to stay motivated is to get started and stay with it until you realize how good you feel that day. People often have trouble getting that motivation because they're looking for longer-term goals like weight loss and being buff and looking good and all that. That will come if you pay attention to how good you're feeling from the exercise itself. Notice how less stressed you are, less anxious you are, less depressed you are.

Variety is very important. I have a patient who's very depressed, and after a really traumatic experience happened in his life, he took up hot yoga three times a week. That led to him, at the age of 55, starting to do muay tai, which is a martial art. He's by far the oldest member of the tribe but he loves it. He's also started to do tai chi. All of this really helped him in his life. His personality wasn't one that was really that open to things, but now it's like he's a completely new person.

Exercise is a whole lifestyle change. Certainly there's the importance of being able to endure exercise, but then we want to look at the many different kinds of exercises. If you are feeling more fit, you're more able to scan the horizon both internally and externally for things you might want to try.

JO: What do people lose by not exercising?

JR: We lose growth. And we start eroding. We say "use it or lose it," and it's true. When you stop thinking or stop moving, your brain is going to erode. The same with your muscles: if you're not using your muscles, they go away. Eventually you won't have the architecture, the muscles, the balance to try things. And you won't be able to experience the joy of movement. The younger you get moving, the better and the more fun you have doing it. Movement is really essential for us, no matter our age.

STICK
TO
A
REALISTIC
TIMEFRAME

Play for Life

HAVE FUN! Do fewer things that suck and more things that bring you joy — just like when you were a kid. Focusing on fun might not sound very serious, but there's a good reason successful people create time for it: The more fun we have, the more we feel truly alive.

What defines fun for you? It could be art classes, salsa lessons, volunteering, board games, meditation, yoga, even cooking up healthier spins on your favourite foods. A preferred activity is an ideal foundation for your new exercise plan — even if it's getting off the bus a stop earlier than normal on your way to art class. If you're doing salsa classes, make your new play activity some dynamic stretching (see page 83) before you leave the house — thinking outside of the box is all it takes!

Again, I can't emphasize enough: *start small*. Small bouts of movement spread throughout the day and week can enhance your mental, physical, and spiritual health, while setting small, realistic objectives can make the biggest impact.

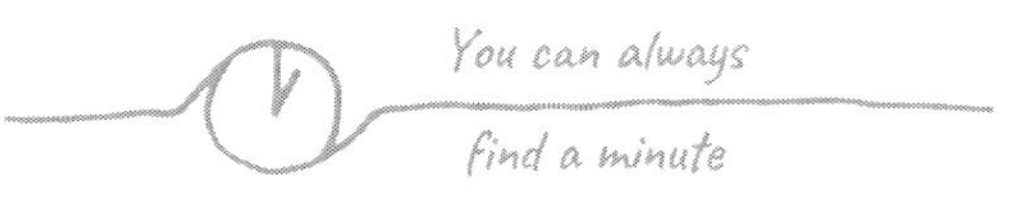

LAUGHING YOGA

In 1995 a doctor in India, Dr. Madan Kataria, began a "Laughter Club" in a park in Mumbai. He had been researching how laughter can benefit the mind and body, including reducing stress and depression. Dr. Kataria learned that the body cannot differentiate between real and fake laughter — you get the same physiological and biological benefits from fake giggles as you do from real guffaws.

From the initial meeting of just 5 people, the group grew to 50 members within a few days, mostly by attracting people passing by who were curious about what was going on. There are now hundreds of members in the happiest communities in the world — there are laughter clubs in over 70 countries.

The movements in most classes are based on clapping, breathing, child-like playfulness, and laughter yoga exercises that deliver more oxygen to the body and brain, making you feel more energetic and healthy. The increased oxygen in the brain decreases stress hormones, improves your immune system, and boosts endorphins. And let's not overlook the wonderful human connection that comes with participating in such a class. You can find out more about this methodology at **laughteryoga.org**.

Get started

How do we figure out what type of play will truly help us feel healthy and happy for the long haul? Start by asking yourself the following questions.

Do I enjoy it?

You don't have to be over-the-top obsessed, but you have to enjoy the activity enough to push past the resistance your mind will give you after the novelty of it wears off. Flip the question and also ask yourself "Do I dread it?" If yes, it's not for you.

Is it sustainable?

An executive with a 70-hour-per-week work schedule is going to have different availability than a college student with a light class load. Even if you love what you're doing, the time commitment has to be sustainable or you'll burn out. Skipping rope for 30 minutes every day or lifting weights for an hour might not be right for you. Start with a time commitment that's without-a-doubt manageable. You can always increase the time later.

> **You can discover more about a person in an hour of play than in a year of conversation.**
> —Plato

I really like how author and habit specialist James Clear explains "inversion" or turning a problem upside down:

> Say you want to start working out. Most people would focus on the lower limit and say "I have to start exercising for at least 45 minutes on Monday, Wednesday, and Friday." Instead, you could turn the problem upside down and say "I am not allowed to exercise for more than 5 minutes on Monday, Wednesday, and Friday." By setting an incredibly easy upper limit, you make the process of getting started and sustaining your behaviour much simpler. Once you establish the routine of doing your behaviour over and over again, you can raise the limit as needed. It is better to make small progress every day than to do as much as humanly possible in one day. Do things you can sustain.

Is there a community of like-minded people to support me?

If you're finding it hard to stay motivated, search out "your people" — others who are interested in or have already started increasing their movement. You can encourage one another, share helpful tips, and generally be a good support and friend to others like you.

Is it working?

Check your progress after 2 months or so. Can you complete your activity faster? Are your legs feeling stronger? Can you manage more stairs without getting out of breath? You can also measure physical markers like body measurements and weight or cholesterol and blood pressure if that's your thing (remember that intrinsic and extrinsic motivation we discussed on page 101?).

PLAN FOR THE LONG TERM

While everyone's strategies are different, try to incorporate the following five guidelines when planning your long-term play habit:

1. Have a great support network and call on them.
2. Never stop learning what works for you. Once you figure that out, keep doing it.
3. There is no finish line. Optimal health and wellness is a life-long process.
4. Focus on behaviours not outcomes. Concentrate on other progress indicators like health, energy, and moving more — and do more of that!

5. You don't have to change, but if you want to there are a lot of tools out there to help you.

Let go of perfection and "end" dates. It's okay when life gets in the way and you have to miss a day. It doesn't mean you are a bad person. It means you are human, and tomorrow is another opportunity to play, which is a mindset sure to keep joy in your life more consistently. Remember: Play is a habit — it's never all or nothing.

Find playmates

Children often create imaginary playmates, but as much fun as that is, as adults we're interested in a different kind of play: increasing our movement. An imaginary friend isn't likely to cut it. However, neither do you need a physical, in-person community. But you should have access to some sort of community. Maybe you really enjoy bodybuilding but love working out alone with your headphones on. Perfect. There are hundreds of bodybuilding forums online where you can learn from and support other people pursuing a common goal. Running and walking can be solitary activities, and maybe you prefer it that way. But with a little research you can find your community online for tips and encouragement.

If you're looking for a running or walking buddy, see if your neighbourhood has a Facebook group and join it to see if anyone wants to walk or run with you. (Heck, join my Facebook community "Play For Life" — I am always here to support your awesomeness.) A dog is great for motivation: just ask my dog, Cooper — there's nothing like those big brown eyes begging me to take him for his daily walk!

Without support, you can feel very isolated, and it's easier to quit when you feel like you're doing it alone.

When my husband, daughter, and I moved to Amsterdam in 1996, I was suddenly in a foreign country with a baby and nobody to play with! I needed to find some like-minded people who were interested in the activities I liked. I joined a state-of-the-art gym with an incredible set-up. They introduced me to a group of people who met every Sunday morning to run together. Joining them turned out to be one of the best choices I made. This group was very encouraging. No one got left behind. Depending on the energy you had that day, there was always someone to run with. In addition, I was encouraged to push myself further than I had in the past: My greatest accomplishment was running the full Amsterdam Marathon before I was 30 years old. The encouragement of my playmates got me there!

> **Exercise because you love your body, not because you hate it.**
> —Unknown

Find a realistic balance

Finding time to spend on activities you enjoy cannot be overstated. But let's be realistic: Sometimes you will feel like working hard and sometimes you will feel like taking it easy. Your mind and body need time to recover — and to find that sweet spot that makes you feel good and happy. The total picture of health has to do with finding the right balance *for you.*

Accept that finding the right play habit involves trial and error, and that whatever you settle on will take a bit of work but that the effort is well worth it. It will bring you one step closer to a lifestyle that helps you be the best version of you. Let's face it: the day-to-day responsibility of our well-being has to come from inside each of us as individuals. We all have to be our own best advocates for our health.

Your success depends partly on two things you already do: eating and sleeping. They're very easy to take for granted, but making them part of your plan, and improving the way you approach them, will make fun and success more achievable.

Get enough rest and sleep

Our bodies are *not* designed to go full tilt 24/7 365 days a year. Rest and recovery matter as much as movement. Our muscles and joints need to recover from the work we ask of them every day. And interestingly, when you increase your amount of play, you'll likely find you sleep better.

You can find many tips on how to get a good night's sleep, but here are a few of my top suggestions in order to get your 7 to 8 hours a night:

- Reserve the bedroom for sleeping. (Not that a bit of romance in the bedroom prohibits a good night's sleep!)
- Keep your bedroom as dark as you possibly can.
- Banish all electronics from the room — you don't want to be tempted to use them but also they won't be giving off that eerie glow that can interfere with a sound, refreshing sleep.
- Try to go to bed at the same time every night.
- Establish a routine so you're relaxed as you turn off the light.
- Keep the bedroom a bit cooler than the rest of the house.

Although our bodies can adapt to stress, too much of it sets off a chain of hormonal and chemical systems that fires up our fight-or-flight mechanisms. Your health and strength will improve if you listen to your body and push it — but not too much. It is a fine balance.

> **Sleep is the golden chain that ties our health and our bodies together.**
> —Thomas Dekker

Fuel your body

Eating well goes hand in hand with rest and sleep to keep your body responding well to your increasingly active life. Sure, you may be starting with just an additional minute at first, then more when you're ready to add some, but after a few months of increasing minutes, your body might start staying, "Hey, give me more fuel to keep me going!" Reaching for a tempting chocolate bar or bag of chips is obviously not the wisest choice. Easy to say, I know, but you'll feel more positive about this new play if you fuel your body with foods that support your desire for good health.

I've talked about the realities of our lives today, that time is always at a premium, but I'm asking you to increase your awareness and be mindful to *eat real food.* If you've relied on packaged, processed, or fast food, consider moving toward more veggies and fruit, whole grains, legumes, olive oil, and nuts, along with nourishing protein (including omega-3-rich fish, such as wild salmon or sardines a couple of times a week).

What you eat determines how well you'll perform.
—Robin Sharma

An excellent resource for getting more greens is over at **halfyourplate.ca**. You'll find an amazing array of videos, ideas, and recipes — new, shared, and fresh takes on old favourites.

The focus of this book is not about nutrition (how you eat, like how you play, is very personal), but what is on your plate matters (depending on your activity level). Here are some things to keep in mind:

- Healthy eating is a mindful, habit-based behaviour like playing and sleeping. When was the last time you knew when you were truly hungry or full?
- Food is meant for fuel and enjoyment — especially with others when you can.
- Meal plan and prep your own food as often as possible.
- Consuming the right portions for your activity level are key to how you use and store energy.
- Learn how to read and understand food labels so that you can grow your knowledge about hidden sugars, saturated fats, and salt. Knowledge is power.
- Hydration is hugely important and so often an overlooked factor when it comes to hunger and energy levels. Figure out how much water your body needs by using this handy formula:

  Your weight in lbs × .55 ÷ 8 = the number of glasses of water to aim for per day

Remember your values

I talked about values in Chapter 2 and recommended that you consider taking time to determine your main motive for moving more, write it down, and keep returning to it. Revisiting your values will keep you on your path. Too often people forget what's motivating them and they stop.

There's a big difference between having a motive ("I want to move more") and being motivated ("You mean I have to do it *now*?"). Think big and make it really fun so it's worth going for day in and day out. Share your excitement with others (friends, family, online support group) as a way of staying committed and motivated, and maybe check back with them daily. Print out pictures and post them somewhere so you are reminded of your favourite play places. You can even create a "vision board" (see page 164) to help remind you of your motivation.

We are bombarded with so many negative images in the media — I call them "psychological barriers to play" — that affect our inner dialogue and our decision to start moving more: unrealistic body images; exercise regimes that seem extreme; images of the elderly sitting around and looking frail. All of these photos intimidate people and prevent them from getting to a fitness facility. Don't let them prevent you from walking out your front door and doing just a bit more every day!

DETERMINE YOUR MOTIVATION

Having a visual to remind you of your goals is a really strong tool to keep you motivated. Follow the instructions on page 128 to make your own motivation board.

RETHINK THE PLAYGROUND

The playground isn't just for kids — you can take advantage of the equipment to incorporate more functional movement into your day.

- ❑ Walk up a slide.
- ❑ Step up (repeatedly) onto a log or bench.
- ❑ Use logs, rocks, or picnic tables to help you do leg raises, calf raises, lunges, squats, stretches — the possibilities are endless.
- ❑ Crawl over or under a bench.
- ❑ Do push-ups on a rock.

Check out **youtube.com/@janetomstead** for videos of these and other ways you can take advantage of your local playground.

Play like a champion

Why is play so valuable? It's an escape from reality that serves to increase our emotional development. It's engaging, non-judgmental, and *fun* without being too sanitized. In play, it doesn't matter if you win or lose. Play is expressive, it's not entertainment. Play is always safe.

With the aim of improving and increasing your movement, play can be what you make it. You might have heard the phrase "play like a champion today." You don't need to be a professional athlete to use that as motivation. Every day, as you continue to practice your movement habit — whether it's simple stretching, a walk around the block, or a swimming session — think of yourself as a champion … a champion at play!

WHAT THE EXPERTS SAY

Lisanne Thomas

Lisanne Thomas is an ACC, PNL2, CSFC, and AACC certified coach specializing in self-care and ADHD. She brings to her heart-centred work a wide-lense perspective in facilitating humans to own and embody their greatness. Prior to founding doingGreat! in 2021 (doinggreat.ca), Lisanne was recruited as a coach by one of the world's largest private nutrition coaching, training, and research companies. For nearly a decade, she provided more than 1,000 clients with individual and group coaching in support of their personal transformations. A personal transformation artist herself, Lisanne followed her passion from a successful career in corporate advertising to being a birth and postpartum doula, childbirth educator, and yoga instructor to business owner and masterful coach.

JO: Why do you think people avoid getting active and what's the biggest barrier that they face?

LT: I don't think we live in a society that values physical activity very much. Since the industrial revolution, we've come to value convenience more. What most of us do day-to-day, especially in our jobs, doesn't require a lot of physical movement, a lot of physicality. Activity isn't convenient in our "first world" kind of lifestyle.

JO: Is there a point at which people will "get it" somehow? Understand why being active is worthwhile?

LT: I think when a person has a sense of accomplishment, then something clicks for them. It's like "Damn, I did that!" or "That felt good" or "I could do this now when I couldn't do it before" — they see or feel or understand that they are capable of doing something that they thought they couldn't. I think that is where the "aha!" comes from — the shift in being motivated. Something changes when it feels like it was out of reach before, and now it's not.

JO: What gets us going in the first place?

LT: I think having an explorer's mind helps — that kind of inquisitive, curious "what could I do here?" style of thinking. It's not a "what *should* I do?" but a "what *can* I do?" And then, perhaps most importantly, observing and celebrating the result.

JO: How can you shape your environment for more play?

LT: I think it's about taking stock of what is actually within your ability to control and what isn't. I'll give you an example. I have this lovely client with a background of really high anxiety, and who lives with a whole lot of family members in the house. They have a shared kitchen, eat different foods, and have no easy access to buying food, so she takes a bus and carries home the groceries. She's doing all this and her family isn't supportive when she asks for time in the living room so she can borrow her brother's weights to do her workout. She doesn't have the physical space in her room to even fit a barbell. Talk about environment! She's not in a conducive environment to change. So my question to her was "What *can* you do?"

In her room she's got a chair — she can do something with a chair. She's got a bed — she can do push-ups on it. Stairs? Walk up and down them — with or without groceries. She can walk outside. I'm asking her to experiment, to find things and ways with what's there that *can* work for her.

JO: How do you get people thinking about the importance of physical movement?

LT: I ask them: How do you want to live? How do you want to show up in the world? Do you want to be able to walk and get your own groceries? Do you want to get down on the floor and play with your grandkids?

I teach yoga at a seniors' home and I see the people that come in. One woman can lift her leg right up — like WOW! She says she does it every morning — right in her bed! One guy leaves his walker in his room because he hates walking around with it. There are people in wheelchairs who can't lift their legs … at all. Somebody has to come by, lift up their legs, and put each footrest up so they can put one foot and then the other on the floor.

JO: Was there a lesson in that for you?

LT: Yeah! If I'm lucky enough to get to that age, I don't want to be the person who needs somebody to come and lift my foot so it can touch the ground. I aspire to be able to move my body however I want to move it. Considering *how* I wanted to live is what helped me change.

I'd also realized I had fallen into the whole convenience of life. I'd go watch my kids play soccer and be, where am I going to sit? You can't stand and watch! You have to go and sit! And get up and go back to the car, and then go pick something up for lunch, and then sit on the couch and watch TV, then go to work and sit down. It felt *very* sedentary. When the kids wanted to go outside and play, I'd be like "Oh, you guys just go and I'll watch!" I realized I didn't want to be that person. And the only reason I was is because I didn't feel comfortable moving my body. I realized that the only way I was going to get comfortable moving my body was if I started moving my body. I think that's true for all of us.

JO: What helped you get more physical activity in your life?

LT: Sometimes exercise has to be on your to-do list! It's one of the tools I used and do use with my clients. But for some, putting something on a list to do was just stressing them out. So, it wasn't getting done, and it wasn't getting done, and it wasn't getting done. Even the idea of structured flexibility — some sort of movement for this amount of time at some point in the day — they just weren't having any of it. So I coach them not to put exercise on the list. Instead, if they *happen* to get something done — like a 10-minute walk or taking a few flights of stairs — then put that on a *ta-da!* list. They record all of their *ta-das!* after the fact, not beforehand.

JO: Can the idea of gamifying help our efforts?

LT: I do love to gamify things. I find something I really want — a little thing — and set a play goal, and when I hit it, I feel like I've earned the right to get it. Another way to play it is "I wonder if I could do this?" Like daring oneself to try something new.

JO: Which exercise or movement is your first recommendation?

LT: I would say definitely the squat. You've got to go to the bathroom, you've got to get in and out of a chair. And just for your whole bowel system, your digestive system, and, for women, pelvic urinary incontinence. Also for women, after childbirth, everyone talks about Kegel exercises, not so much about squatting, The squat complements Kegels well to strengthen the pelvic floor muscles.

JO: Why is intentional movement important?

LT: I will be physical throughout the day, but when I'm not intentional about my movement then I don't know *how* I'm moving. It's that inner assessment — how am I squatting right now? How does my shoulder feel as I turn? If I'm not tuning-in on a semi-regular basis to how my body feels or is functioning, I could get hurt. I could bend over to get something and throw my back out because I don't have any sense of what's going on.

Beyond that, by paying that kind of attention, it's less likely that one day I'll suddenly notice how I look or how I move (or don't move or can't move!) and go "Oh my, when did *that* happen?" For a lot of people that's exactly what happens. It's because they're not willing to see what's there. But when you are faced with what *is,* you have the opportunity to make the decision to do nothing about it or do something.

Think of the trajectory: If I keep on as is, what will my body look like 10 or 15 years down the road? What would it look like if I just did these little things? Moving this way … playing that way?

PLEASE.
LOOK.
AFTER.
YOURSELF.

There's really no doubt about it: Moving your body consistently can dramatically enhance your quality of life by improving your heart, functional ability, and mobility, not to mention your mental health. Moving your body in a way that brings you joy will make establishing a habit of play even easier.

So, c'mon, try something new. What makes *you* feel good? What gives *you* energy? Experiment. Ask yourself if your own self-doubt is holding you back. If weight and looks weren't values of measure, what would you do? If you got rid of that all-or-nothing attitude, what might you try? How would a shift in mindset transform the way you show up in life?

"Health offers amazing freeedom that once gone, is often gone forever." Wise words from Bronnie Ware, the bestselling author of *The Top Five Regrets of the Dying* (who also happens to be a nurse).

Commit to making a change, if only a small one at first. Establish your BAM and work up from there, including plenty of low-intensity aerobic daily movements to help with endurance, circulation, and longevity (getting to that 20 minutes) — it can be as simple as fidgeting, doing housework, walking the dog, standing to talk on the phone. Stack on some fundamental movement patterns a couple of times a week: push, pull, rotation and level change/squat. Strength keeps your muscles powerful and your body coordinated.

As long as you keep showing up — consistently — you can be active and functional in a way that you love, for life. I know you'll be happier for it.

150 WAYS TO MOVE MORE

1. Take the stairs
2. Walk home
3. Walk your dog
4. Jump rope
5. Step on the cracks in the sidewalk
6. Park further from your front door
7. Mow your lawn (and your neighbour's)
8. Stop using drive-throughs
9. Sit/stand up/sit down on a chair slowly
10. Sit/stand up/sit down on a bench
11. Sit/stand up/sit down on a rock
12. Jump over an object
13. Pick up sticks in your local park or even your yard
14. Carry your groceries
15. Row with soup cans
16. Push up on a park bench
17. Do tricep dips on chair
18. Ride your bike
19. Fly a kite

20. Take 5 deep belly breaths
21. Walk outside
22. Do some gentle stretches
23. Balance on one foot for as long as you can then switch
24. Go for a run
25. Stand up super slowly
26. Take a walking meeting
27. Stroll in the park
28. Dance to some music
29. Play the (air) drums
30. Try laughing yoga
31. Sweep the driveway
32. Shovel the snow (and your neighbour's)
33. Squat while brushing your teeth
34. Take two stairs instead of one
35. Squeeze your butt while you chop veggies
36. Walk on your tiptoes
37. Jump up and touch the doorframe
38. Play tug of war with your kid and/or pet
39. Hop over a bench and crawl under
40. Hold the door open for someone
41. Dance in the elevator
42. Weed the garden

43. Try hula hooping
44. Use a standing desk
45. Walk during your lunch hour
46. Take a post-dinner walk
47. Stretch during TV commercials
48. Stand up when speaking on the phone
49. Do some jumping jacks
50. Squeeze a tennis ball
51. Play hide and seek
52. Touch your toes
53. Spend time in nature
54. Kick a ball
55. Fidget more
56. Try geocaching
57. Go on a scavenger hunt
58. Explore a new neighbourhood on foot
59. Go bowling with friends
60. Try golf at a driving range
61. Do standing pushups on the counter while dinner is cooking
62. Try indoor rock climbing
63. Take up nature photography
64. Go bird watching
65. Sit against a wall

66. Start an office soccer/softball/tag team
67. Try a mid-morning stretch
68. Take up gardening
69. Coach a sports team
70. Participate in a charity walking event
71. Do bicep curls with your grocery bags or shopping bags
72. Take up basketball
73. Shoot hoops with your kids
74. Try aquafit
75. Brace your abs for 10 seconds
76. Stand straight
77. Do yoga
78. Stand when using technology
79. Play frisbee
80. Go hiking
81. Take up fishing
82. Sit on the floor
83. Do pushups after you pee
84. Hold a baby
85. Try the monkey bars at the playground
86. Climb up a slide at the playground
87. Sit up straight
88. Hand wash the dishes

89. Get off the bus a stop earlier
90. Walk and talk with your friend
91. Make your bed
92. Get rid of your couch
93. Install a pull up bar in your doorframe
94. Kneel in church
95. Do the twist
96. Do arm circles
97. Roll your shoulders
98. Stretch your arms in a doorframe
99. Stand on a book to stretch your calves
100. Massage your feet
101. Play tag with your kids
102. Sign up for a fitness class
103. Do squats while you check your phone
104. Jump the lines in a parking lot
105. Walk the mall
106. Walk on treadmill while watching TV
107. Vacuum to music
108. Try seated calf raises
109. Hold a warrior pose
110. Pick up 5 pieces of garbage when walking
111. Stretch before bed

112. Try paper plate lunges
113. Go snowshoeing
114. Rest your legs up on a wall
115. Do a handstand
116. Squeeze your shoulder blades together
117. Watch something funny standing up
118. Brush your cat
119. Hand wash your car
120. Go sailing
121. Tread water
122. Try a standup paddle board
123. Bungee jump
124. Toss a ball
125. Play kick the can
126. Crawl like a baby
127. Chase your dog
128. Puddle jump
129. Balance on a rock
130. Stand on one foot
131. Extend your legs in seated position
132. Rake the leaves
133. Split your own wood
134. Try inline skating

135. Scooter to the store

136. Walk backward

137. Sidestep up stairs

138. Make a playdate

139. Pick flowers

140. Cut the hedges with shears

141. Pick up a heavy object

142. Skip down the street

143. Go rowing

144. Walk uphill

145. Try tai chi

146. Learn to juggle

147. Take samba lessons

148. Pole dance

149. Try zumba

150. Go skateboarding

PERSONAL ASSESSMENTS

I've developed the following assessments to be a catalyst for you to add more play to your life, in both the short and long term. They are intended to help you get to know yourself better as you read the book by asking questions, some of which you may not have considered before. Here you can work through your thought processes to sort out the answers, discern what you are comfortable starting with, and make better decisions that you'll find easier to keep up with. I recommend working through them one at a time, in the order presented.

If you prefer to work digitally, you can download these assessments at **janetomstead.com**.

Personal Assessments

ASSESSING MOTIVATION: ARE YOU READY?

This section will help you work through your thoughts about becoming more active and help you prepare for action.

OVERCOMING THE BARRIERS: ARE YOU SET?

This section will help you start to take action and set you up for success.

SUPPORT STRATEGIES: LET'S GO!

This section will help you maintain play/movement for life.

①

Identify Your Core Values

Change is more likely to stick when you choose something that is consistent with your higher values. What you identify as your core values will help guide you toward what you are most passionate about when it comes to play. Your values drive your emotions and will help you make the decisions that matter for your daily personal play journey. They are the reasons you show up in life every single day.

Values silently guide our action. Like using a map or a GPS to help get you to your destination, your values drive your motivation to move forward or hold you back in fear. When you understand who you are and where you are going, it is easier to decide the path you want to take day in and day out. Your values can change over time, but understanding what you value deepens your understanding of what is truly inspiring you. Values make life and play meaningful.

Here is a list of values. Choose three to five that speak to you personally (feel free to add any you don't see here) and write them on the following page.

achievement
adventure
appearance
authenticity
authority
balance
belonging
boldness
challenge
community
compassion
competence
competition
contribution
courage
creativity
curiosity
education
empathy
environment
exercise
excellence
fairness
faith
family
forgiveness
friendship
fun
growth
happiness
health
helping
honesty
humour
integrity
leadership
love
loyalty
intimacy
kindness
knowledge
neatness
optimism
openness
peace
perseverance
persistence
personal growth
play
pleasure
power
prosperity
rationality
recognition
respect
security
self-control
self-respect
selfishness
stability
teamwork
tolerance
tradition

What three to five values are the most significant to you?

1. ______________________________
2. ______________________________
3. ______________________________
4. ______________________________
5. ______________________________

With those values in mind, can you establish a sentence or two that aligns your values with your play mission? Here's an example:

> I value my health. Play is a way to combine my sense of adventure and community with taking care of my family. I want to continue personally growing in this area.

Your turn:

____

____

____

____

____

②

Remember How You Used to Play

If you are struggling to move enough during the day, sometimes it helps to brainstorm other ways you can fit activities into your day. How did you love to play when you were young? Start there. Begin by listing the things you like to do in the chart below. Then list what you *dislike* — you don't have to do those activities ever again. When considering your list, ask yourself: "Do these align with my values?"

Ideas:

Bike

Walk

Swim

Take an exercise class

Participate in a team sport

Play with your friends

Skip rope

Things I Like Doing

Things I Don't Like Doing

3

Track Your Play

Try some form of play and commit to doing it for 2 weeks at first. Keep it simple to start and something you can guarantee will make you happy. If you find what you chose doesn't make you happy, change it — there are no rules, only tools to help you go from inactive to active in your own time. You don't have to wait until Monday to start.

Fill out the following "play tracker" and colour in the play buttons as you go. Consistency matters most — keep showing up until you are playing the way that suits your life. Only add in a new habit once the first one is well established.

You can download this template at janetomstead.com and print it out or try an online tracker such as **strides.com**. Whichever method you choose, keep it visible and track your progress daily.

Play happens one day at a time. What will you do?

Play Tracker

Fill in a play button every time you show up to play — there's a button for every day of the year!

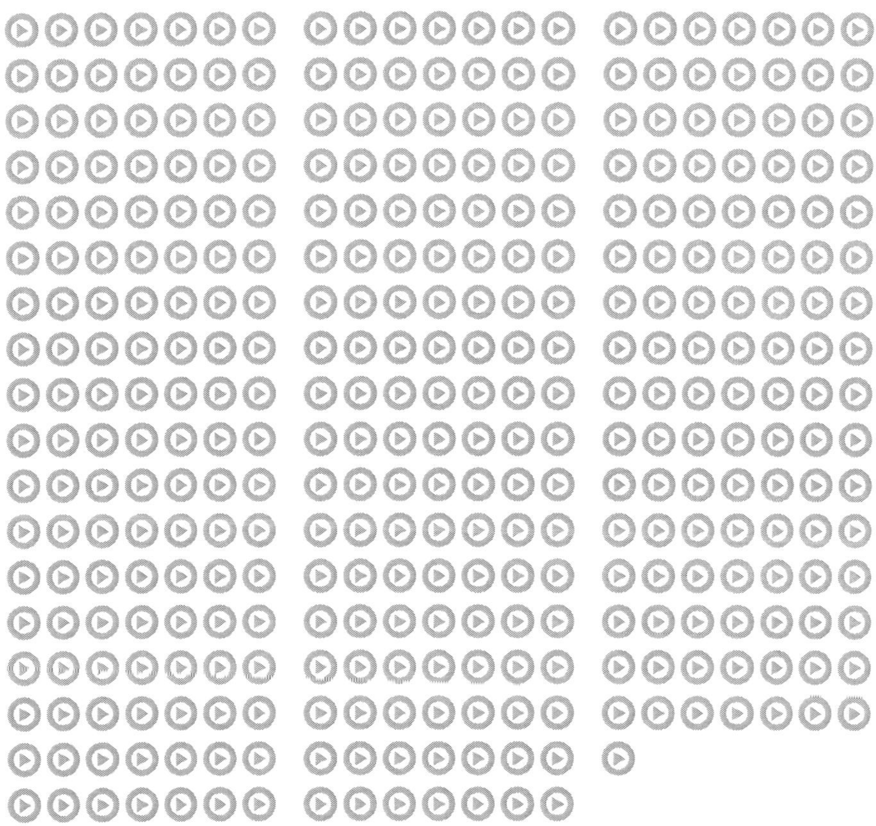

4

Find Your Time-Out

You may think you don't have any time to play, but there's a way to find your lost minutes in a day. This task is meant to show you where your time is going or how you may be giving priorities to everything else except your health.

Let's work through your average day and find where there are opportunities for more movement. Feel free to record more than one day if your days are not typically the same.

Once you've determined some patterns, you will clearly see where play activities could fit into your schedule. Then you can make a plan accordingly.

Time	Activity	Position (Sit, stand, lie down, etc.)
5:00 a.m.		
5:30		
6:00		
6:30		
7:00		
7:30		
8:00		
8:30		
9:00		
9:30		
10:00		
10:30		
11:00		
11:30		
12:00 p.m.		
12:30		
1:00		

Time	Activity	Position (Sit, stand, lie down, etc.)
1:30		
2:00		
2:30		
3:00		
3:30		
4:00		
4:30		
5:00		
5:30		
6:00		
6:30		
7:00		
7:30		
8:00		
8:30		
9:00		
9:30		
10:00		

Time	Activity	Position (Sit, stand, lie down, etc.)
10:30		
11:00		
11:30		
12:00 a.m.		
12:30		
1:00		
1:30		
2:00		
2:30		
3:00		
3:30		
4:00		
4:30		
5:00 a.m.		

5

Choose Your 5-Minute Function

When you think of your own reality, ability, and current lifestyle, what small actions could you take *right now* to move you closer to your own play goal? The World Health Organization recommends doing strength exercises 2 days a week in addition to cardio. Using the basics — push/pull/squat/rotation movement patterns — how creative can you get?

Often	Sometimes	Not Likely Ever
Walking	Running	Sprinting
Walking the escalator	Taking the stairs	Jumping lunges
Standing more	Squats	Deadlifts
Push-ups on wall	Pushups from knees	Clapping push-ups
Sitting up straight	Row with a band	Pull-ups
Sweeping the floor	Standing twists	Side planks
Taking 5 deep breaths	Meditation	Hot yoga

Often	Sometimes	Not Likely Ever

6

Understand Your Limiting Beliefs and Super Powers

Our beliefs determine our actions and our success. Whatever you believe will be true. A limiting belief system or "no way" mentality is disempowering and can create fear, anger, frustration, or resentment. A growth or "what if" mindset, on the other hand, is empowering and creates love, gratitude, acceptance, and optimism. What can you let go of to move from a fixed mindset to a growth mindset (see page 54)? In order to see really good results, keep flipping the perspective.

In the chart below, write down what you think is limiting your ability to become healthier in the left column. In the right column, list the opposite — what things will help you get on track and squash your negative self-talk? In other words, what things are preventing you from taking that first step? I've provided some examples to get you started.

No way ***(limiting beliefs)***	**What if?** ***(empowering)***
No time	Find 5 minutes
So tired	How can I add movement into my current schedule?
	Take the stairs, park further away etc.
Too old	Invite a friend to join in
Hate gyms	The World is your playground.
	All I need is right outside my door or in my own living space.

No way ***(limiting beliefs)***	**What if?** ***(empowering)***

7

Determine Your Motivation

Have you ever thought about what motivates you? Is it a friend who goes on active holidays, a family member who walks their dog daily, a neighbour who is always gardening? A simple but effective way to lay out your own ideas of what motivates you is to create a motivation board (see example on next page). Or, you can do this online and create a page in an App like Instagram — rather than making it public, you can make it private — or Pinterest is a good one, too. Add a daily photo/quote for visual motivation.

1. Discern your intentions.

What do you want? What do you need? What do you value? (Refer to Assessment 1 where you identified your core values.) And how do you want to feel when those things are made manifest? When thinking of the feelings, be sure to choose single emotion words like *free, open, joy,* etc. Write them down.

2. **Gather your supplies.**

- blank poster board/a large sheet of paper, and/or a cork board
- glue/pins
- markers, pens, paint
- colourful or plain paper
- magazines/books/printed-out images that can be cut up
- scissors

3. Find your images and words.

Flip through the magazines and begin tearing/cutting out images/words/phrases that appeal to you.

4. Paste them to the board — physically or online.

Go through your images and words, looking specifically for things that reflect the feelings of your intentions, and start arranging them on your board. When it feels just right, go ahead and attach them to your board. Set aside any images that still feel good but don't quite fit what you are going for. You can use them in future pages or boards.

Be sure not to choose images that send you into "compare and despair" or that otherwise make you feel crappy! (Believe it or not, it's one of the biggest mistakes people make with vision boards.)

5. Put your vision board somewhere you can see it.

Your vision board can now be used as a visual reminder of what you are working toward in your life. Look at your board often and connect with why you created it. Mine is on my bathroom wall!

6. Write a "make it real" list.

Make a list of the things you could experiment with to start living out your values *now.* That's the awesome thing about using your values to guide you — you can be successful now, without waiting for something external to change.

Be sure to ground your list in things that you are actually in control of. If you are already doing things that feel the way you want, make note of that, too. Get as specific as you can and start choosing those things as often as possible.

7. Notice and heal any resistance.

As you begin making your visions real, you may start to notice resistance in the form of stories, thoughts, and patterns that are getting in the way of you making a change. Spend time examining them, thinking about them, so you can heal and move closer to what you want.

8. Repeat.

Continue to check in and ask yourself how things are going. Make adjustments and keep fine-tuning. Trust the process and remember: You wouldn't be able to dream it if it wasn't a possibility.

Afterword to this Reissued Edition

As Walt Disney famously said, "The way to get started is to quit talking and begin doing."

You now have all the tools to make play a habit, and it's time to start doing!

The first step is to come up with an action plan. Your action plan is a broader, more long-term strategy. Goals are great but implementing systems will help you achieve subsequent actions.

Then you need to arm yourself with *both* an actionable plan and a sound strategy. Think of it as having an overall game plan. The game is life, and it's meant to be the one you win while having fun! There are two parts of a game plan to consider:

Part 1: Set your GPS

Do you have a clear sense of where you're at and a meaningful sense of direction? You need clarity and awareness around your values and priorities (see page 149) and to understand your deeper motivation (see page 164). Ask yourself:

- ***Where are you right now?*** Review your baseline and where you're starting from.
- ***Where do you want to go?*** Identify the main objectives.
- ***What are you working with?*** Assess the situation.
- ***How are you going to do what you're going to do?*** Determine your overall approach and method.
- ***What are you going to do?*** Identify a general set of potential skills, practices, and actions.

Part 2: Have a backup plan

- ***What happens if things go wrong?*** Anticipate obstacles and develop backup plans.
- ***How will you know if your plan is working?*** Track your progress using the play tracker on page 155.
- ***What are you going to do first?*** Decide on your action steps. What exactly is your game plan?

You can call on this backup plan to boost yourself during challenging times and supply a vital source of intrinsic motivation (see pages 100 to 101) to help you stay the course. Motion creates motivation!

To create an effective game plan, you can use the simple FITT Formula tool that follows. FITT stands for *Frequency, Intensity, Time,* and *Type.*

FITT FORMULA

Frequency refers to how often you exercise.

Intensity refers to how hard you exercise.

Time refers to how long you exercise.

Type refers to the kind of exercise you do.

FITT is the foundation of any play program. Think of it this way: Your doctor will prescribe a particular type of medication at a specific dosage, to be taken a certain number of times each day, and for a certain period of time. Your play prescription works the same way.

As a play expert, I use this tool to help create movement programs for my clients. You can write your own play prescription by following the steps outlined below.

Many people fail to make sustainable progress in their health because they forget to keep things simple. For any play program to be effective, each of the FITT principles must be considered and understood.

Let's look at each of the FITT components in a little more detail:

Frequency is a crucial component of the FITT principle because you need to adjust the number of times you exercise per week to reflect your current level of health, the time you realistically have available, your other commitments (like family and work), and the goals you've set for yourself.

Intensity is essential to the FITT principle and is the hardest to monitor. The best way to gauge the power of your play is to monitor your heart rate (like I mentioned on pages 38 to 41). The simplest way to monitor intensity is to use the "talk test." The harder you play, the faster you become breathless and the harder it becomes to talk. You're performing at an intense level if you can talk but not sing. You will begin to breathe faster and have difficulty talking as you walk faster. At that point, you've achieved moderate or "somewhat hard" intensity. If you take a beta-blocker or any other medication that affects your heart rate, exercise at an intensity that you feel is "somewhat hard."

The **time** you dedicate to play usually depends on the type of play undertaken and your current experience level. If you are newish or restarting a playing habit, start small with your BAM (I feel like a broken record when I say that, but it matters; see pages 34 to 36). Since time is a limiting factor for many people, don't forget that all movement matters and that the recommended 20 minutes a day can be broken up into smaller increments that fit your schedule (see page 32).

The **type** of movement you choose to get your heart pumping (aka cardio) is up to you, as well as how to incorporate the four pillars of functional movements (as discussed on pages 69 to 71) and which days you set aside for recovery (see page 82).

SUPER IMPORTANT NOTE

I can't stress this enough: Talk with your doctor before you begin any play program. If you have been inactive for a long time, start with short sessions and build from there.

You will not be able to go from 0 to 100 in the next few weeks. The goal is to increase your activity level slowly and safely and make it fun. Being 50 to 75% consistent day in and day out far outweighs making 100% effort for only two weeks.

Once you have determined your motivation and come up with a specific game plan, putting your play habit into practice can be as simple as it is practical. Playing will be the driving force behind better health in the long run and the ability to fight chronic disease as you age.

Need help? Contact me via **janetomstead.com** and let's get playing.

THANK YOU

This manuscript has been shaped and molded by many key players. Saying "thank you" to those without whom this book would never be in your hands just doesn't seem to express my feelings nearly enough. I am so grateful to the following people for all of their help.

Thank you to Shawn, my husband: You always support and encourage me to believe that anything is possible. I love you so very much.

Thank you to my kids, Meredith and Jack: Through thick and thin you are my forever playmates — I feel so lucky to be your mom.

Thanks to Janice Biehn, my best friend from camp, who over 15 years ago first planted the seed for me to write a book: "Hey, Jan. You *totally* need to write a book about play!"

Since then I've made many connections to find the right people to help me bring this book to life, including one with my good friend Peter Neal, who introduced me to his awesome editor, Tracy Bordian. (Thanks, Pete!) Tracy understood my "vision" and has had endless patience and spent countless hours over two years helping me turn the pages of my manuscript into a book I'm super proud of. Thank you to Tracy and her team: Rob Scanlan for his design expertise; Wendy Thomas and Eleanor Gasparik for editorial support; and Christopher Rouleau for bringing my "play line" to life with his drawings.

The years I spent in television production and research helped me feel comfortable reaching out to the experts: Dr. Krista Scott-Dixon, Dr. Paul Oh, Juan Carlos Santana, Cindy Gorlewski, Dr. John Ratey, and Lisanne Thomas. Each of them agreed to be interviewed for this book. I am humbled by your leadership and selflessness. Thank you.

I have learned so much from being "on the playing field" with my awesome clients as well as my friend and LifeSports business partner, Kym Grippo. I appreciate your support and friendship.

Much of what I've incorporated in this book has been inspired by my continued education, particularily my Level 1 and Level 2 Coaching Certifications (as well as Internship) through Precision Nutrition, without which I could have never done justice to the topics of psychology and the power of habit-based change.

Special thanks to my crew of friends who took the time to review different versions of the book: Susanne (Spookie) Fletcher, my Mom, Dr. Carmine (Carm) Filice of The Performance Lab, my kids, and Omer.

Thanks as well to those who read an advance copy of the book and provided their testimonials, including Peter Neal, Brian Shelley, John Shannon, Tracy Wilson, Paula Morand, and David Kincaid.

Big thanks to my friend Adam Growe for writing the Foreword.

I hope that I have inspired you to move your body. Do what you like, like what you do, and I guarantee you will find success. Take a class, join a club, schedule your time. Show up … it will be worth it. You are either living or you're dying. Get off the bench and get out there and play!

BIBLIOGRAPHY

AARP. "This Is Your Brain On Play." Accessed at: https://lifereimagined.aarp.org/stories/3441-This-Is-Your-Brain-On-Play

Babauta, Leo. *The Power of Less: The Fine Art of Limiting Yourself to the Essential … in Business and in Life.* New York: Hachette Books, 2009, pp. 26, 41, 160.

Bennington, Vanessa. "It's Not Your Metabolism, It's Your "NEAT" That's Stopping Your Fat Loss." 2017. Accessed at: https://breakingmuscle.com/fitness/its-not-your-metabolism-its-your-neat-thats-stopping-your-fat-loss

Brodwin, Erin. "14 Ways One Type of Exercise Is the Closest Thing to a Miracle Drug We Have." March 19, 2018. Accessed at: https://www.businessinsider.com/exercise-cardio-brain-body-health-benefits-2017-12

Buettner, Dan. *The Blue Zones: Lessons for Living Longer form the People Who've Lived the Longest.* Washington, D.C.: The National Geographic Society, 2008, p. 229.

Carrol, Aaron E. "Closest Thing to a Wonder Drug? Try Exercise." *The New York Times*, June 20, 2016. Accessed at: https://www.nytimes.com/2016/06/21/upshot/why-you-should-exercise-no-not-to-lose-weight.html

Cherry, Kendra. "A Guide to the Anatomy of the Brain." Updated May 14, 2019. Accessed at: https://www.verywellmind.com/the-anatomy-of-the-brain-2794895

Clear, James. "Motivation Is Overvalued: Environment Often Matters More." July 7, 2016. Accessed at: https://jamesclear.com/power-of-environment

Clear, James. *Atomic Habits.* New York: Penguin Press, 2018, pp. 16, 24.

Clear, James. "3 Simple Ways to Make Exercise a Habit." September 18, 2014. Accessed at: https://jamesclear.com/exercise-habit

Clifford, Dawn, and Curtis, Laura. *Motivational Interviewing in Nutrition and Fitness.* New York: The Guilford Press, 2016, p. 213.

Dotson-Renta, Lara N. "Why Young Kids Learn Through Movement." May 19, 2016. Accessed at: https://www.theatlantic.com/education/archive/2016/05/why-young-kids-learn-through-movement/483408/

Duggal, Niharika Arora, et al. "Major Features of Immunesenescence, Including Reduced Thymic Output, Are Ameliorated by High Levels of Physical Activity In Adulthood." *Aging Cell,* vol. 17, 2 (2018): e12750.

Goldberg, M.E. "Parietal Lobe." *International Encyclopedia of the Social and Behavioral Sciences* 2001. Accessed at: https://www.sciencedirect.com/topics/neuroscience/parietal-lobe

Gray, Peter. "The Value of Play 1: The Definition of Play Gives Insights." *Psychology Today,* November 19, 2008. Accessed at: https://www.psychologytoday.com/blog/freedom-learn/200811/the-value-i-the-definition-play-gives-insights

Hallal, Pedro C., et al. "Physical Activity: More of the Same Is Not Enough." *The Lancet,* July 18, 2012. Accessed at: https://www.thelancet.com/journals/lancet/article/PIIS0140-6736(12)61027-7/fulltext

Harvard Health Publishing. "5 of the Best Exercises You Can Ever Do." March 1, 2017. Accessed at: https://www.health.harvard.edu/staying-healthy/5-of-the-best-exercises-you-can-ever-do

Heid, Markham. "Why Weight Training Is Ridiculously Good For You." *Time Health,* June 6, 2017. Accessed at: http://time.com/4803697/bodybuilding-strength-training%C2%A0/?platform=hootsuite

Jackson, Elizabeth A. "The Physical Activity Guidelines for Americans." American College of Cardiology, last modified November 14, 2018. Accessed at: https://www.acc.org/latest-in-cardiology/ten-points-to-remember/2018/11/14/14/37/the-physical-activity-guidelines-for-americans

Lamonte, Michael J. "Accelerometer-Measured Physical Activity and Mortaility in Women Ages 63 to 99." *Journal of the American Geriatrics Society,* November 16, 2017. Accessed at: https://onlinelibrary.wiley.com/doi/full/10.1111/jgs.15201

Lowen, Alexander. AZQuotes.com, Wind and Fly LTD. March 11, 2018. Accessed at: https://www.azquotes.com/author/19015-Alexander_Lowen

Mayo Clinic. "Aging: What to Expect." November 21, 2018. Accessed at: https://www.mayoclinic.org/healthy-lifestyle/healthy-aging/in-depth/aging/art-20046070

Northey, J.M., Cherbuin, N., Pumpa, K.L., et al. "Exercise Interventions for Cognitive Function in Adults Older Than 50: A Systematic Review with Meta-Analysis." *Br J Sports Med* 2018 (52), pp. 154–160. Accessed at: https://bjsm.bmj.com/content/52/3/154

Nowak, Achim. "When We Hit the Play Button." *The Moment Expert,* August 13, 2018. Accessed at http://themoment.expert/2018/08/13/when-we-hit-play/

Oaklander, Mandy. "The New Science of Exercise." *Time Inc. Special,* April 28, 2017, pp. 12, 21.

Patton, Meiko S. "How to Improve Your Self-Esteem and Self-Image: The Postage Stamp Method." September 7, 2017. Accessed at: https://www.huffingtonpost.com/entry/how-to-improve-your-self-esteem-self-image-the_us_59b1b121e4b0c50640cd65e0

Ratey, John J. "Run, Jump, Learn! How Exercise Can Transform Our Schools." Filmed November 18, 2012, at TEDxManhattanBeach, Manhattan Beach, CA. Video, 0:2:55.00. Accessed at: https://www.youtube.com/watch?time_continue=18&v=hBSVZdTQmDs

Ratey, John J. *SPARK: The Revolutionary New Science of Exercise and The Brain.* New York: Little Brown, 2008, p. 5.

Reynolds, Gretchen. "The Right Dose of Exercise for a Longer Life." *New York Times*, April 15, 2015. Accessed at: https://well.blogs.nytimes.com/2015/04/15/the-right-dose-of-exercise-for-a-longer-life/

Santana, Juan Carlos. *Functional Training: Exercises and Programming for Training and Performance.* Windsor, ON: Human Kinetics, 2016, p. 5.

Scientist Staff. "How We Age: From DNA Damage to Cellular Miscommunication, Aging Is a Mysterious and Multifarious Process." March 1, 2015. Accessed at: https://www.the-scientist.com/features/how-we-age-35872

Sharma, Robin. *The Leader Who Had No Title.* New York: Simon & Schuster, 2010, pp. 181, 185.

Swart, Tara. "4 Habits You Didn't Know Were Holding Back Your Brain Performance." December 20, 2017. Accessed at: https://www.forbes.com/sites/taraswart/2017/12/20/4-habits-you-didnt-know-were-holding-back-your-brain-performance/#5c2490dc398d

Ware, Bronnie. *The Top Five Regrets of the Dying: A Life Transformed by the Dearly Departing.* NY: Hay House Inc., 2011, p. 172.

WebMD. "Sarcopenia With Aging." Reviewed by Carol DerSakissian. July 30, 2018. Accessed at: https://www.webmd.com/healthy-aging/guide/sarcopenia-with-aging#1

World Health Organization. "Physical Activity and Adults." Accessed at: https://www.who.int/dietphysicalactivity/factsheet_adults/en/

World Health Organization. "Physical activity Fact Sheet." Accessed at: https://www.who.int/news-room/fact-sheets/detail/physical-activity

INDEX

D

E

F

N

O

P

ABOUT THE AUTHOR

Janet Omstead is an author, speaker, personal trainer, elite behaviour-change health coach, and play expert. With over 20 years of experience in the health and wellness industry, Janet's strength lies in working with individual and corporate clients to make sustainable progress toward optimal health while having fun.

After surviving three near-death experiences, Janet has embraced life by playing her mission. This positive mindset has seen Janet through the ups and downs of raising kids, being a caregiver as her husband battled Leukemia, recovering from injuries and accidents, and losing loved ones. It's also enabled her to embrace some amazing opportunities such as interviewing famous athletes, travelling the world singing on the stage at Carnegie Hall (twice), and, most of all, helping others live healthy, full, vibrant lives.

Janet knows there is no one-size-fits-all approach to health. Using her PLAY method, she coaches busy people who want long-term, sustainable solutions with their movement, nutrition, and stress management. Janet keeps you on track and inspired, even when the going gets tough, for results that last a lifetime.

LET'S PLAY FOR LIFE!

Sign up for my newsletter
janetomstead.com

Connect with me on:

Instagram
@janetomstead

LinkedIn
linkedin.com/in/janetomstead

Get coached!
Book a complimentary discovery call and let's see if we are a good fit to work together.
janlovestoplay@gmail.com